D0955386

BEING ENOUGH

ALSO BY CHIEKO OKAZAKI

Lighten Up!

Cat's Cradle

Aloha

Sanctuary

Disciples

BEING ENOUGH

Chieko N. Okazaki

BOOKCRAFT

SALT LAKE CITY, UTAH

© 2002 Chieko N. Okazaki

All rights reserved. No part of this book may be reproduced in any form or by any means without permission in writing from the publisher, Deseret Book Company, P. O. Box 30178, Salt Lake City, Utah 84130. This work is not an official publication of The Church of Jesus Christ of Latter-day Saints. The views expressed herein are the responsibility of the author and do not necessarily represent the position of the Church or of Deseret Book Company.

Bookcraft is a registered trademark of Deseret Book Company.

Visit us at deseretbook.com

Library of Congress Cataloging-in-Publication Data

Okazaki, Chieko N., 1926–
    Being enough / Chieko N. Okazaki.
        p.   cm.
    Includes bibliographical references and index.
    ISBN 1-57008-876-4 (hardbound : alk. paper)
        1. Christian life—Mormon authors.   2. Mormons—Religious life.   I. Title.
BX8656 .O38 2002
248.4'89332—dc21   2002010705

Printed in the United States of America   72076-300094
Publishers Printing, Salt Lake City, Utah

10   9   8   7   6   5   4   3   2

To Kenzo, my grandson

CONTENTS

I

Being Enough

—————   —————

t a challenging moment in Church history, the Lord gave this inspiring commandment to the Saints: "Arise and shine forth, that thy light may be a standard for all nations" (D&C 115:5). What I would like to focus on are those moments just before arising and shining forth, when your light feels pretty dim and you don't feel much like a standard of anything. I want to do this because I think we need to understand how brightly our light shines in comparison with our moments of weariness and discouragement. All too often we compare our light with our very brightest moments or with someone else's brightest moments, and it makes the darkness deeper around us.

In a day when there seem to be almost overwhelming demands on us to do more, to do it faster and better, and to be more things to more people, I want to explore how much oil we need in our lamps. I want to explore "being enough."

For me, this is a much needed message of hope, for it is easy to be discouraged in the face of demands that always escalate, that never diminish. And so, there is great hope and encouragement and comfort in the message: Who you are is enough. What you have to give is enough. Your best is sufficient. Your light shines enough to be a standard.

Let's begin with a story that on the surface seems to be about poverty but is actually about abundance. It's important to understand the context. It may have been Jesus' last public sermon. He had entered Jerusalem on the back of a donkey while the multitude sang praises to God and spread their cloaks and palm fronds over his path. He went into the temple and drove out the merchants, then he taught in the temple, surrounded by people who clustered close, famished for the word of life, but also surrounded by the sharks of the priests, the teachers, and the Sadducees. His enemies tried to trick him by asking him whether baptisms performed by John the Baptist were valid, whether they should pay taxes, and whether there would be a resurrection from the dead. In response, Jesus told them a parable of the evil-doers who rejected each messenger from the absent king and finally, when he sent his own son, killed him. Jesus warned that the temple would be destroyed and that a time of persecution was coming.

In the midst of these turbulent events and as his own life was rapidly drawing to a close, Jesus "looked up, and saw the rich men casting their gifts into the treasury. And he saw also a certain poor widow casting in thither two mites. And he said, Of a truth I say unto you, that this poor widow hath cast in more than they all: For all these have of their abundance cast in unto the offerings of God: but she of her penury hath cast in all the living that she had" (Luke 21:1–4).

In drawing attention to the contrast between the rich givers and the poor widow, Jesus was also pointing out the difference between those who listened to him willingly and those who listened only to find fault, between those who wanted to kill him and those who found in him great hope. He was stressing the difference between appearance and reality—

identifying hypocrisy where he encountered it and calling on the people to turn to God.

We usually praise the widow for her sacrifice: that she gave everything, putting her own life in jeopardy so she could make a contribution. I see in Jesus' praise of this poor widow a joyous acceptance, even a celebration of her gift. He attested that her offering was not only enough, but was incredibly generous, unbelievably abundant. What she had to give was enough and more than enough.

With that in mind, I would like you to consider three commodities that we often think we don't have enough of: power, love, and time. Before you do, however, I want to point out that we sometimes confuse *having* enough with *being* enough. I'll come back at the end of this chapter to the concept of *being* enough, but my hope is that if I can persuade you that you *have* enough power, love, and time, it will be easier for you to believe that you *are* enough.

Enough Power

Let's talk first about having enough power. Sometimes it startles women to be involved in a discussion of power, but let's face it: when you feel powerless as a mother to protect your children, when you feel powerless as an employee to command a living wage, when you feel powerless as a wife to improve your marriage, when you feel powerless at church or in the community to have a voice—then it's pretty easy to feel that you are not enough.

In Jewish society, powerlessness was practically the middle name of widows. They were defined by what they didn't have—a husband. Furthermore, Jesus could tell at a glance that this woman was a "poor" widow. So she was defined by two things she didn't have: she didn't have money and she didn't have a husband. Jeni and Richard Holzapfel have described the plight of the widow in those times:

"Most [widows] lived a precarious existence since their major source of protection and identity, their husband, was dead. While sons, other male relatives, or family wealth could provide a measure of security, widows were traditionally considered subjects of special moral concern because of their generally defenseless legal and financial position in ancient society. . . . A widow was not only disadvantaged by poverty but also by her vulnerable status as an unmarried woman, thus rendering her practically invisible in the legal, political, social, and religious eyes of first-century Jewish society."[1]

I think many women can relate to this view of being defined as someone "without." If you are single, you are a woman without a husband. If you are widowed, like me, you are a woman without a companion. If you are divorced, you are a woman without a celestial marriage. If you are married to a less active member or to a husband who is not a member of the Church, then you are a woman without priesthood in your home. If you do not have children, you are a woman without motherhood. If you don't have the right number of children or the right kind of children or children who are properly behaved, then you are a woman without something that all Mormon women everywhere are somehow, magically, supposed to acquire.

If you are employed outside the home, you are without quantity time to spend with your children. If you are not employed outside the home, you are without some of the skills, social connections, professional development, and personal satisfactions that come from those experiences. And let's not even get started on the situation of being without enough money! Every TV commercial is a reminder of cars you don't have, furniture you are lacking, food you are not eating, and clothes you don't have in your closet.

Let's look again at the poverty of that widow Jesus saw. She cast two mites into the treasury. They were the smallest coins in circulation in Palestine, and their real name was lepta. The lepton was a bronze coin worth 1/400 of a shekel—between an eighth and a fourth of a penny. Two lepta were not enough to pay for a simple meal.

So this woman, who could not buy herself a bowl of stew or a piece of bread and cheese, was still bringing what she had to the Lord's temple. But remember what Jesus said about her? "This poor widow hath cast more in, than all they which have cast into the treasury: For all they did cast in of their abundance; but she of her want did cast in all that she had, even all her living" (Mark 12:43–44).

So which, of the two, manifested generosity? Who really had abundance? It was this woman upon whom the world looked as a woman without, a woman who did not have enough, a woman who basically had nothing at all. Jesus was probably the only person in all of Jerusalem who looked at this woman and saw that she had given with abundance—and fortunately, his is really the only opinion that counts.

We don't know how the widow felt. We don't know if she lingered to hear Jesus speak or if she hurried away, hoping nobody would notice her. We don't know if she ever heard the message of hope and empowerment in the gospel. Golda Meir, the first woman prime minister of Israel, said that she spent whole years feeling stretched so thin and so inadequate to the tasks before her as a mother, wife, national leader, and policy maker that she went to bed every night asking herself, "Who or what have I neglected today?"[2] This is a question that kills the heart. As Emma Lou Thayne—poet, mother of five, and former member of the Young Women's general board—explains: "I too always wanted more. But I cannot go back. . . . We do what we can, we are what we are. To expect more of ourselves is to be mired in discouragement if not despair, the most unproductive of sentences for anyone. We're all basically paddling to stay afloat the best way we know how. With no two of us ever mustering in the same way, how we do it is more to be understood than criticized."[3]

Now, sisters, if for any reason at all you have defined yourself as a woman without or let someone else define you as a woman without, I implore you with all of the energy and love that I have to see yourself as Jesus sees you. See yourself as a woman who has such an abundance of love, such an abundance of generosity, such an abundance of trust and faith that you can give all, every minute of every day, knowing that if you receive Jesus, you will in return receive the "Father's kingdom" and "all that [the] Father hath" (D&C 84:38). Can you want more than that?

If the generosity of the widow seemed incredibly reckless, remember the promise of the Lord: "Cast thy bread upon the waters: for thou shalt find it after many days" (Ecclesiastes 11:1). If you feel afraid of others, remember that the Lord "preparest a table before me in the presence of mine enemies: thou anointest my head with oil; my cup runneth over" (Psalm 23:5); and "The Lord is my rock, and my fortress, and my deliverer; my God, my strength, in whom I will trust; my buckler, and the horn of my salvation, and my high tower" (Psalm 18:2). And if you feel powerless, remember the Apostle Paul rejoicing, "I can do all things through Christ which strength-eneth me" (Philippians 4:13).

It is probably true that our own wisdom is inadequate, our own love too quickly exhausted, our own patience in short supply, our own resources too scanty, our own capability too limited, our own talents too stunted. But the good news of the gospel is that we are not alone.

This mortal probation is not a test of any of those things. It is an invitation to walk with faith with the Savior, and his promise is that he will make up all of our deficiencies. That's what grace means. That's what grace is for. If we will give Christ our trust, then he will provide everything we lack, "good measure, pressed down, and shaken together, and running over" (Luke 6:38).

The prophet Haggai rebuked the people with a description of scarcity, saying that the Lord had this message for them: "Now therefore thus saith the Lord of hosts; Consider your ways. Ye have sown much, and bring in little; ye eat, but ye have not enough; ye drink, but ye are not filled with drink; ye clothe you, but there is none warm; and he that earneth wages . . . put[s] it into a bag with holes. Thus saith the Lord of hosts; Consider your ways" (Haggai 1:5–7).

Why were these ancient Israelites fighting a losing battle with scarcity? Why did their best efforts never yield enough? It was because their way was not the Lord's way. They had not considered his way, the way of righteousness. Instead of receiv-ing food and drink from his hands with gratitude, they had grasped in greediness and need and anxiety—and there wasn't enough. They had poured their efforts into projects that had not paid off. Their clothes did not warm them; their money did not bring them security.

Let me suggest instead that we pray, as Alma says to pray, over every relationship, over every place we put our effort, over our in-comings and our out-goings. Let us weave a conversation with God into our daily lives every day and let him weave the wonderful words of his own back into our lives. If we accept his invitation to become his yokefellow, then we won't be surprised when we suddenly start making progress.

Let me share with you the experience of Sister Carolyn Wold, who was serving with her husband in a very difficult area of Russia. She had been feeling discouraged but saw things in a new light after she read something I had written, and she wrote to thank me. She said:

"Having devoted much energy and devotion in helping our missionaries over the past year, I turned my attention to the needs of the members. Now that we know 'the lay of the land' so to speak, we could see and understand things more clearly, and the problems and challenges we face have loomed up like giant elephants ready to stomp us out.

"The 'need' bank in this part of the world is a bottomless pit, and our efforts to help, teach, orient, etc., seem minuscule in comparison. I found myself sinking into despair. Maybe if we implemented one more program, visited one more branch, taught another leadership class, etc., etc., we might make a difference. I was feeling guilty because we only spent twenty-four hours a day focused on the mission instead of twenty-five! . . .

"I found myself kneeling in prayer telling the Lord that everything was too much, and that I was no match for the challenges in this country. I even doubted that our call was inspired and had come to view it as some awful mistake with our names coming up in a computer somewhere. . . .

"Then a remarkable thing happened [after I read a message

from you.] . . . I found myself plainly placing the overwhelming challenges and seemingly insolvable problems right at the feet of our Savior. He has a plan and a timetable for this country that is beyond my capacity to comprehend. I want desperately to be an instrument in His hands—'the little pencil'—but He must do the writing. I can't even write the alphabet by myself, and I have been trying to write volumes.

"As I placed my burdens at His feet, I replaced them with the seemingly small joys that are here in abundance. The darkness was gone. In being able to do this, a freshness of pure light poured into my soul. I can mother eighty-six missionaries. This is something that has brought me great joy. We have the greatest young men and women here in our mission. It was even impressed upon my mind at one time that future General Authorities would come out of this mission. I can, as a partner with my husband, enjoy the many small miracles and joys that happen on a daily basis and take comfort knowing that 'out of small things proceedeth that which is great' (D&C 64:33). I can love my children, and I resolved to write home about my happiness and the truths I am learning. Perhaps it will have an impact on their lives. And I can love the Russian members on an individual basis and enjoy their love as they reciprocate to me. These things I do and do reasonably well and enjoy. The rest belongs to the Lord."[4]

It wasn't my words, of course, that prompted this new feeling of empowerment and joy. It was the Lord's words, and I'm just grateful that I had been able to bear my testimony of them in a way that the Spirit could bear witness to Sister Wold. But the important thing is her testimony to you—that the feeling of despair and powerlessness can give way to a powerful feeling of joy and freshness and a willingness when we let the Lord help with the burden he is so anxious to carry.

I think as women we tend not to pay attention to the need to be personally empowered—which is sort of like denying there are mosquitoes while we keep wondering where all these itchy bumps are coming from. I hope I've persuaded you that the Savior offers real power—lasting power, shared power, his power—if we will only reach out to him with trust and confidence.

Enough Love

Now let's consider the second point. Having enough love. I have a testimony that our ability to love comes from the Savior. He is the prime example of love, and I believe our willingness to be enlarged by love comes in large part from our appreciation of the infinite plenitude of his love for us.

We live in a world that is held together by love—organized by love, maintained by love, and nurtured by love. Ultimately it will be redeemed by love, and even now it is in the process of being redeemed by the love and kindness that we offer each other. A philosopher I much admire once said:

"A favorite argument of those who disagree with the idea of a purposeful God is to point to all the evil in the world. 'How can a benevolent God,' they ask, 'permit so much badness to exist and flourish?'

"I always like to answer this question by turning it inside out and confronting these people with what I call 'the problem of good.' How do they account for the existence of so much good in the world? How is it that man, who a few thousand years ago was on the level of the beasts [sacrificing his own children to idols and enslaving those who were less powerful than he], has risen to the heights of love, unselfishness, and self-sacrifice? Why should he lay down his life for his friend? Why should he sacrifice his welfare for others? Why has the history of humanity been so illuminated by heroes and martyrs who have willingly died for an idea greater than themselves?

"We tend to take for granted the virtues of mankind and to excoriate its vices. But why should mankind have any virtues beyond those of the scorpion or the spider? We have far more cause for rejoicing at God's goodness than for reviling man's imperfection."[5]

In other words, even when it looks as if the world is full of evil and menace, it is not so. It is easy to understand why mankind would naturally be selfish and exploitative; so why are so many people kind and loving? That's the real puzzle. And we can contribute to increasing the amount of love in the world.

The Apostle Paul hinted at these exciting possibilities when he made this promise to the Corinthians, which I've adapted slightly so that it applies particularly to women:

"But this I say, [she] which soweth sparingly shall reap also sparingly; and [she] which soweth bountifully shall reap also bountifully.

"Every [woman] according as [she] purposeth in [her] heart, so let [her] give; not grudgingly, or of necessity: for God loveth a cheerful giver.

"And God is able to make all grace abound toward you; that ye, always having all sufficiency in all things, may abound to every good work" (2 Corinthians 9:6–8; adapted).

In other words, we have sufficient because grace abounds. If good works abound in us, it is not because we are so great but because God is so great. Our ability to love is small, but his love fills the universe. Every loving word we speak has his accent in it. Every loving gesture we make mirrors the movement of his hands. Every loving thought we think was first in his mind. Clearly, there is no way we can run out of love. The source of love is inexhaustible. But he works through human channels for much the same reason that we water our lawns with a sprinkler instead of with a fire hose. His love is a secret that we each have to learn for ourselves. Just opening the fire hydrant on humanity would wash away quite a few. So Jesus asks us to transmit that love in quiet, gentle ways that will nurture without damaging others but which will let people feel curious about the source of that love until they seek it themselves.

Church history records a beautiful story of late July 1839 when the Saints were trying to settle Nauvoo. Many of them were very ill because of malaria, and Joseph Smith went throughout the settlement blessing the sick. He crossed over the Mississippi River to Montrose, Iowa, directly opposite Nauvoo, where many of the Saints were also suffering, and healed them. Then this incident happened:

"After healing the sick in Montrose, all the company followed Joseph to the bank of the river, where he was going to take the boat to return home. While waiting for the boat, a man from the West [evidently not a member of the Church], who had seen that the sick and dying were healed, asked Joseph if he would not go to his house and heal two of his children who were very sick. They were twins and were three months old. Joseph told the man he could not go, but he would send someone to heal them. He told Elder Woodruff to go with the man and heal his children. At the same time he took from his pocket a silk bandanna handkerchief, and gave it to Brother Woodruff, telling him to wipe the faces of the children with it, and they should be healed; and remarked at the same time: 'As long as you keep that handkerchief it shall remain a league between you and me.' Elder Woodruff did as he was commanded, and the children were healed, and he keeps the handkerchief to this day."[6]

Now, there is nothing magical or miraculous about the silk fabric of the Prophet's handkerchief, but there is something miraculous about love—about the love of a prophet for an anxious father and his babies, about that prophet's love for the messenger of healing whom he sent with a commission and a promise of an undying bond between them.

Enough Time

We've considered having enough power and having enough love, and now we come to having enough time. This life is all the time we have, and each of us has exactly the same amount of time in every day: rich or poor, married or not, sick or well, we each have a steady succession of minutes and hours making up each day of our life. And the worst thing we can do is to give away the time we have by living in either the past or the future because there's not one blessed thing we can do to alter the past or to make the future arrive any faster.

So the way to have the most possible time is to live each moment as fully as we can, being completely present. If we are talking to someone, let's listen with our full attention, not with half of our mind planning what we're going to cook for dinner. If we're singing a hymn, let's enjoy every note. If we're giving someone a hug, let's rejoice in that embrace.

"If we are ever to enjoy life, now is the time—not tomorrow, nor next year, nor in some future life after we have died. The best preparation for a better life next year is a full, complete, harmonious, joyous life this year. Our beliefs in a rich future life are of little importance unless we coin them into a rich present life. Today should always be our most wonderful day."[7]

If we're living in the moment, we can respond to the moment appropriately, as this mother's experience shows:

"It was a hot afternoon, and my eight-year-old son, Zeb, ran off to play with his friends Mike and Devin. What walked into the kitchen a couple hours later was a body Zeb's size covered with mud. In his ears, his nose, his hair, around his eyes, the stuff was all over him.

"Although my mouth dropped open, words momentarily failed me. When I found my voice, I asked in amazement, 'What did you do?'

"'Oh, we were just playing in some mud,' Zeb answered with classic understatement.

"I wasn't sure if I should lecture him or laugh. So I drew him a bath instead, hoping the wisdom for an appropriate response would come to me soon.

"As the tub was filling, Zeb said, 'Mike was in big trouble when his mom saw him.'

"'What did she say?' I asked, feeling a kinship with Mike's mom.

"'You get in here right now!'

"I stifled a laugh. . . . Devin was being cared for by his grandma that day, and I asked how she had responded to the awful sight. Zeb smiled . . . 'She said, "Wow! You're a master-piece!"'

"And suddenly it was my heart's prayer that, before he's fully grown, I'll . . . respond to my son's childhood as wisely and as lightly as Devin's grandma. At least, occasionally."[8]

If we don't have time for masterpiece moments, the very reason we came to earth is being wasted on us.

Conclusion

I hope you've had some concepts and insights come to you about the ways in which you have enough: enough power, enough love, enough time, enough light that you can arise and shine forth.

Remember the poor widow who is a symbol of abundance because of her love and trust. Remember Sister Wold in Russia, laying her burden of what she could not do at the Savior's feet and feeling the freedom of enjoying all the rest of what she could do.

Remember that the source of power for us is Christ himself, who reminds us over and over that his grace is "sufficient," even "abounding." Whatever we need, he has sufficient for us. Christ is also the source of love for us. We love him because he first loved us and showed us what that love meant through his atonement.

And third, remember that we each have all the time there is, all that anybody has. But it is given to us by God who stands outside of time and who literally can give us eternity. Choose where to spend your time. Remember Zeb and his muddy masterpiece. Choose to celebrate such moments.

If there have been times in the past when you have felt like a woman without—whether that perceived deficiency is not enough time, not enough talent, not enough children, not enough respect, not enough ability—please follow the example of the widow whom Jesus commended: give all you have, all that you may have already consecrated. In prayer each morning, consecrate anew the moments of that day and the desires of your heart and your gratitude for your blessings, and you will feel yourself expanding to receive the love and promises and blessings that our Heavenly Father has prepared for you, and you will walk and work that day with the companionship of the Holy Ghost.

Take comfort in the Lord's wonderful assurance:

"Fear not, little children, for you are mine, and I have overcome the world, and you are of them that my Father hath given me;

"And none of them that my Father hath given me shall be lost.

"And the Father and I are one. I am in the Father and the Father in me; and inasmuch as ye have received me, ye are in me and I in you.

"Wherefore, I am in your midst, and I am the good shepherd, and the stone of Israel. He that buildeth upon this rock shall never fall.

"And the day cometh that you shall hear my voice and see me, and know that I am" (D&C 50:41–45).

Already we can hear whispers and catch glimpses and feel intimations of that perfect knowledge stirring in our hearts. May we live to realize that blessing.

NOTES

1. Jeni Broberg Holzapfel and Richard Nietzel Holzapfel, *Sisters at the Well: Women and the Life and Teachings of Jesus* (Salt Lake City: Bookcraft, 1993), 97.

2. Quoted in Emma Lou Thayne, *As for Me and My House* (Salt Lake City: Bookcraft, 1989), 46.

3. Ibid.

4. Carolyn Wold, Russia Samara Mission, Letter to Chieko Okazaki, July 4, 1997.

5. Sidney J. Harris, "Strictly Personal." Pasted onto p. 74 of a *Readers Digest* article in my possession.

6. *History of the Church of Jesus Christ of Latter-day Saints, Period I* (Salt Lake City: Deseret Book, 1974), 4:4–5.

7. Thomas Dreier, "[untitled note]," *Voice for Health*, May-June 1995, May-June 1995, 17.

8. Ellyn Baumann, *Daily Guideposts, 1994* (Carmel, New York: Guideposts, 1993), 168–69.

2

APPLES IN A SEED

There's a story about Groucho Marx attending a party in Hollywood. At the end, he found his hostess, shook her hand, and said very sincerely, "I've had a wonderful evening. But this wasn't it." I hope that the time spent reading this chapter will not leave you feeling the same way, but rather that you will feel we've shared something important from our hearts and our spirits.

As I think about what characterizes people who have a hopeful and optimistic outlook on life, I think I can summarize it in two short mottoes. The first is "Start over!" The second is "Carry on!" At first glance, these two ideas may seem contradictory, but they're really not.

Let me illustrate. If you cut an apple open and slice it into six or eight parts, it is quite easy to count the number of seeds it contains. If we're careful and accurate, there's no doubt at all about the final figure.

But imagine this. If we were to take a seed from that original apple and plant it, carefully nurturing and tending it so that it sprouted and then sent up a shoot and then became a sapling, it would eventually become a young tree with leaves, blossoms, and fruit. Can you calculate how many hundreds of apples such a tree might bear during its lifetime? Multiply that by each of the seeds in that original apple and what might you have? There could potentially be trillions!

So it's easy to count how many seeds there are in an apple, but perhaps only our Father in Heaven can count how many apples there are in a seed. Each tree, each apple, and each seed can be seen as a new beginning. But each tree, each apple, and each seed can also be seen as a continuation of all the apples, seeds, and trees that have gone before it. So let's consider both ideas: the idea of continuity, and the idea of beginning anew.

Carry On

First, think about continuity. My son Ken and I spent Christmas in Greece a few years ago. It was a wonderful opportunity for us. As I stood on the Parthenon and walked among the ancient buildings that provided a setting for democracy more than two thousand years ago, I felt humbled and honored to be in the presence of those very stones. We were there with a friend who teaches Greek literature. She told us stories from Greek mythology—I recognized those same plots in today's soap operas—and together we read translated quotations from some of Greece's classical philosophers and playwrights about beauty, truth, honor, democracy, and justice.

I exclaimed to my son, "They were just like we are!" Then I realized, No, we are just like *they* were. Our traditions of jurisprudence, law, and high ideals come, at least partly, from ancient Greece. That moment of emotional contact, at a time when we were in physical contact with the artifacts from their past, was an experience I will never forget. I thought, *Here am I, American by birth and upbringing, of Japanese ancestry, raised in Hawaii on the other side of the globe, and yet I recognize that, in very tangible ways, these ancient Greeks are my spiritual and intellectual ancestors.* It was a moment of very real connectedness that made me realize how important it is to recognize continuity in our lives. We are enriched when we feel ourselves connected to the past—to the past of our nations, to the past of our families, and to those parts of our personal pasts that make us strong.

In his first press conference as president of the Church, President Gordon B. Hinckley was asked what counsel he might have for members of the Church. He replied simply, "Carry on!" That is in harmony with the scriptural injunction to "endure to the end" and with what the Lord told Joseph Smith: "And behold, I, the Lord, declare unto you, and my words are sure and shall not fail, that . . . all things must come to pass in their time. Wherefore, be not weary in well-doing, for ye are laying the foundation of a great work. And out of small things proceedeth that which is great" (D&C 64:31–33).

I have always liked it very much that the Japanese character that means "results" is formed from the Chinese pictograph for a tree bearing fruit.[1]

Every woman in the world knows a lot about well-doing that is also sometimes wearisome. We know about doing small things in the hope that they will be the foundation of greater things. Each woman who has children or who has taught children knows how it feels to teach simple skills, simple ideas, and simple principles over and over and over to the same child, and then over and over and over to the next child. It takes a special kind of toughness and freshness combined to find joy in the process each time and not to become weary in this well-doing.

Housekeeping is exactly the same kind of activity. Claudia Bushman wrote once that housekeeping was one of those activities that is invisible, unless it's *not* done. Many church callings are also in this category. Few people may notice that you have played the piano for the Primary children every Sunday for three years—until you catch the flu. And often it's easy to overlook the fact that the Sunday School secretary faithfully passes out rolls, collects them, and compiles the reports every week and every month and every year. It's invisible labor, until it doesn't get done, and then *everybody* seems to notice and have an opinion about it.

I'd like to thank you for all of the quiet steps forward you have taken to persist in well-doing, whether anyone has noticed them or not. I'd like to ask you, sincerely and humbly, to continue in well-doing and in doing good. It may not be for many years, it may not even be in this life, that you will understand how great and glorious your works truly are.

How many of you have daily contact with children—your own or someone else's? How many of you also have weekly contact with at least one or two other people with whom you share a task? This may be in your employment or it may be in community service or in your church callings. I am asking you to build strength and continuity and high quality into those relationships, a little at a time, day by day, and even moment by moment.

Someone once commented, "We do not remember days, we remember moments."[2] How true this is! And because we are human beings—eternal beings spending some time in mortality where, by definition, we have very short attention spans—I think the best way to concentrate on the things of eternity is to treat each moment as though it contained eternity. Maybe your heart sinks at the idea of being cheerful while undertaking a boring task for a whole morning. That's all right. Try being cheerful for a moment. Maybe you can't promise to be patient for the entire year your child is two. That's all right. You can be patient for a moment, and then for another moment, and then maybe for the moment in between that links the first two moments.

There's a Japanese proverb, "*Ari no ana kara tsutsumi mo kuzureru*," which means, "Enough ant holes will make a mountain fall down." There may be particular moments and particular gifts in which you are called to move a mountain with a gigantic earth mover, all yellow and roaring and dramatic. But the faith that moves mountains is equally willing to work with an ordinary pick and shovel.

So try being an ant hole. Try remembering that you only have to rise to the occasion for a moment. And if you rise to that occasion and then have a down moment, don't be hard on yourself for not suddenly being able to stop being human. Jesus came to us in our humanness. He didn't demand that we perfect ourselves and then present ourselves for inspection before he would deign to notice us. Henry Ward Beecher said, "Find the thing meant for you to do and do the best you can. You must be faithful to the place where God put you and for which you are equipped."[3] There is much in our society that tells us that "duty" and "responsibility" are not very glamorous. No, frequently they're not. They're something better. They're glorious!

When I was a little girl my mother taught me how to make a cake. We didn't have an oven. We had a shiny square tin box that we put over our little kerosene fire. It settled over the flame and trapped the heat within it, but you didn't have any way to judge the temperature inside except by experience and by regulating the heat very carefully. It was pretty tricky, but I worked hard and thought I had learned how to do it. The first time I made a cake completely on my own, without my mother's supervision, I was about eight years old, and the cake was pretty experimental. I didn't know how to adjust the fire, and the cake burned on the bottom. And it didn't just scorch a little. About one-fourth of the cake was completely black.

I was so disappointed and ashamed that I had made such a serious mistake. "Oh," I wailed to my father, "I was supposed to make this cake for your supper." My dad took my feelings seriously, even if he didn't take the cake very seriously. He said, "That's okay. I'll show you how to fix it." He took out the bread knife and cut off the bottom and said, "We'll throw this part away and look! What we have left is a very fine cake."

My parents raised us children with kindness and acceptance. There was no scolding, no judging. I never heard them complain about or criticize other people, even when my mother received tremendous pressure from my father's mother. And perhaps you know how much power the mother-in-law has in oriental society. My mother's sister-in-law was also very harsh to my mother, but she looked beyond the stress of the moment and turned those disappointing moments into peaceful, happy moments by letting the feelings go past her. In the same way, my father turned my disappointing moment with the cake into a happy moment for both of us.

Can you do the same with the children in your lives? And also do the same with the individuals with whom you must work? I am asking you to be consistent in building high-quality moments into your relationships with children and into your relationships with colleagues because both of these relationships tend to get focused easily on the job at hand, on the task, on the work, and on the sheer maintenance aspects. But you will know other areas in your life where such attentiveness is appropriate.

The scriptures refer to this quality in a couple of different ways. On the occasion when Jesus fed the four thousand with seven loaves and "a few little fishes," he expressed his concern for the people by calling together his disciples and saying, "I have compassion on the multitude, because *they continue with me* now three days, and have nothing to eat: and I will not send them away fasting, lest they faint in the way" (Matthew 15:32; emphasis added). Maybe you've wondered what it would have been like to be in the presence of Jesus during one of his great miracles, like the miracle of the loaves and fishes. I'm sure it was a wonderful moment. But I wonder what it would have been like to have "continued with" Jesus for three days before that. I'm sure there were many wonderful moments, but "continuing with" means that those wonderful moments were interspersed with fatigue and discomfort from sleeping on the ground, and physical hunger to the point that Jesus knew they would faint if they started back to their homes without food.

Our commitment to Christ requires us to continue with him. There won't be miracles of loaves and fishes every day, but there *will* be miracles for those who "continue with" him during the preceding days of teaching and searching for under-standing. I wonder if this is the feeling the Psalmist wanted to communicate when he prayed to the Lord, "O *continue* thy lovingkindness unto them that know thee; and thy righ-teousness to the upright in heart" (Psalm 36:10; emphasis added).

As a third area, I also ask you to be consistent in your rela-tionship with the Lord. Sir William Osler once commented, "Nothing in life is more wonderful than faith—the one great moving force which we can neither weigh in the balance nor test in the crucible."[4]

President Gordon B. Hinckley tells a very touching story about a naval officer he met from a distant nation. The young man was brilliant and had been brought to the United States for some advanced training, where he came in contact with some Latter-day Saint men who shared with him the message of the Restoration. Though he had previously not been a Christian, he embraced the gospel and was converted and baptized.

When this young man was introduced to President Hinckley, the prophet said to him, "Your people are not Christians. What will happen when you return home a Christian, and, more particularly, a Mormon Christian?"

The man's face clouded, and he replied, "My family will be disappointed. They may cast me out and regard me as dead. As for my future and my career, all opportunity may be foreclosed against me."

President Hinckley then asked, "Are you willing to pay so great a price for the gospel?"

"His dark eyes, moistened by tears, shone in his handsome brown face as he answered, 'It's true, isn't it?'

"Ashamed at having asked the question, [President Hinckley] responded, 'Yes, it's true.'

"To which he replied, 'Then what else matters?'"[5]

You remember that Father Lehi, in speaking to his way-ward sons, told Lemuel: "O that thou mightest be like unto this valley, firm and steadfast, and immovable in keeping the commandments of the Lord!" (1 Nephi 2:10). It is interesting to me that exactly the same phrase appears twice more in the Book of Mormon. The second time, King Benjamin, in teaching his people, tells them: "Therefore, I would that ye should be steadfast and immovable, always abounding in good works, that Christ, the Lord God Omnipotent, may seal you his, that you may be brought to heaven, that ye may have everlasting salvation and eternal life, through the wisdom, and power, and justice, and mercy of him who created all things, in heaven and in earth, who is God above all" (Mosiah 5:15). And a third time, following the appearance of the resurrected Lord, after the righteous generations have passed away and the people are beginning to be wicked again, it is recorded that "the church was broken up in all the land save it were among a few of the Lamanites who were converted unto the true faith; and they would not depart from it, for they were firm, and steadfast, and immovable, willing with all diligence to keep the commandments of the Lord" (3 Nephi 6:14).

Firmness, steadfastness, immovability—these are wonderful qualities in the context of continuity, when we are trying to understand the meaning of "Carry on!" I am not exaggerating when I say that our ability to be optimistic as we face the future rests absolutely on our commitment to "carry on."

Start Over

But if the commitment to "Carry on!" is so great, how can it also be important to "Start over!"? Aren't these two messages contradictory? No, there are some things we cannot carry on without starting over again and again. Each act of repentance is simultaneously a new beginning and also a drawing on the continuity of our faith and testimony of the Savior's love. Each time we partake of the sacrament, we are _re_newing our covenants with the Savior, which represents the continuity of our commitment to him. But do you remember the words of our hymn, "Come, let us anew our journey pursue" (_Hymns_, no. 217)? We always pause after "anew" to take a breath at the line break, but if you read it as poetry, it's all one thought, and it means, "Come, let us pursue our journey anew (or again)." The wonderful thing about the gospel is that it gives us as many chances to renew and anew as we need. And we need them every day.

The prophet Ezekiel urged his people to seek a new heart. "Cast away from you all your transgressions, whereby ye have transgressed; and make you a new heart and a new spirit: for why will ye die, O house of Israel? For I have no pleasure in the death of him that dieth, saith the Lord GOD: wherefore turn yourselves, and live ye" (Ezekiel 18:31–32).

And the Lord himself, speaking through Ezekiel, renewed this same promise: "And I will give them one heart, and I will put a new spirit within you; and I will take the stony heart out of their flesh, and will give them an heart of flesh: That they may walk in my statutes, and keep mine ordinances, and do them: and they shall be my people, and I will be their God" (Ezekiel 11:19–20).

I wonder what the Lord will say to those of us with hard hearts, who have turned our faces away from the suffering of others. If we are in comfortable circumstances, if we have strong marriages, if our children are happy and healthy, then these are blessings that should make us strong enough to give, not treasures to be hoarded like a miser for fear that something will break in and take them from us.

Since the Relief Society's sesquicentennial in 1992, many thousands of Relief Society sisters have made wonderful contributions to their communities in a variety of ways. This is as it should be. Emily H. Woodmansee, a member of the Relief Society general board about the turn of the century, wrote a

poem, set to music by Evan Stephens, expressing the commitment of Mormon women to great causes. I found it in the 1927
hymnal. It reads:

> Oh! Daughters of truth, ye have cause to rejoice.
> Lo! the key of advancement is placed in your keeping,
> To help with your might whatsoever is right,
> To gladden their hearts who are weary of weeping.
> By commandment divine, Zion's daughters must shine,
> And all of the sex, e'en as one, should combine;
> For a oneness of action success will ensure
> In resisting the wrongs that 'tis wrong to endure.
> O woman! God gave thee the longing to bless:
> . . . And not in the rear, hence, need woman appear;
> Her star is ascending, her zenith is near.
> . . . There is blessing in blessing, admit it we must,
> And there's honor in helping a cause that is just.[6]

Community service and brotherly and sisterly service
within our wards and stakes is part of the picture, but on a
more personal level the desire for new beginnings should burn
in each of us. I love the principle of repentance. It tells me
simply that I can be a better, stronger, happier person today
than I was yesterday and that tomorrow will be even better. If
there are things in my life that I am doing wrong, I pray to be
shown what they are so that I can change and come closer to
the Savior. There is an old Chinese proverb that says, "No possible rearrangement of bad eggs can ever make a good omelet."[7]
Sometimes you just have to clean out the pan and start over.

And an old family proverb comes from my mother, who
used to tell us children, at the beginning of each school year,
"Begin well and do not fear the end." We understood the

courage she was giving us to face a change that might be a challenge. But she was also telling us that we can't always control or predict the end from the beginning. We have to move forward in faith, being sure that each step is done with integrity and faith and love and that it is worthy to be done for its own sake.

We cannot fear the end because we do not know when the end will come. And we can never, as members of the Church, say that the end justifies the means. We simply don't know what the end will be. And my feeling is that even a good goal can be contaminated and corrupted by bad means. Be honest. Be faithful. Do the best you can at all times.

We don't know when the world will end, if you want to take the most extreme example. We don't know when Christ will return. We don't know when our own lives will end. We don't know when the life of someone close to us will end. We don't know when our circumstances will change, due to forces over which we have no control. That means that we can never do anything shoddy or morally questionable in the belief that the end will justify it, because we simply have no control over the end.

It is my firm belief that people who plant trees and sow seeds are not people who are suddenly attracted by change for its own sake or who act on a whim or who suffer from low impulse control. Nor are they stick-in-the-muds, who are comfortable in a rut and who don't want change.

Rather, these are people who have long experience with planting in hope and nurturing in faith, waiting for the harvest with quiet confidence. They have imagination enough to visualize the oak tree in the acorn and the flower in the seed. They have faith that God has in store for them even more

wonderful surprises than those they can imagine for themselves. They are people who see the apples in the seed, as well
as those who see the seeds in the apple.

Conclusion

Remember how we began? With Groucho Marx saying
he'd had a wonderful evening but this wasn't it? I hope we've
been able to think, with a light touch and a fresh perspective,
about the serious matter of making new beginnings that still
carry on the good things from the past with continuity.

When you think of carrying on, remember the apple and
the finite number of seeds it contained, but also the infinite
number of apples contained in each seed. Think about being
consistently faithful in little things, even when they weary you.
Think about making each moment one that has some eternity
in it. Remember my mother, patiently showing me how to
bake a cake in our hot box, and my father, cutting off the
burned bottom when it didn't turn out perfectly. Think about
the moments when you can show increased love and patience
to the children in your life and to those who work with you on
shared tasks.

Remember those who continued with Jesus and were present at the miracle of the loaves and fishes during the final
moments of those three days. Remember the valley of Lemuel
and the exhortations from the Book of Mormon to remain
"steadfast and immovable" in keeping the baptismal and
temple covenants you have made. Remember also President
Hinckley's young friend who was able to be steadfast even
when it appeared that he would lose other important things in
his life due to his faithfulness to the gospel.

Then think about new beginnings. Think about Ezekiel,
transmitting the promise of the Lord that his people would

have their stony hearts replaced by a heart of flesh. Think about areas of your personal life that need to be changed or about contributions that you could make to your ward, your neighborhood, and your community by reaching out in new ways. Think about planting trees and sowing seeds, even though the world, or your personal world, seems to be ending. And think about the renewal that comes each Sabbath day from partaking of the sacrament in the trust and hope and love of the Savior that each day can be a new beginning.

Let me share with you a beautiful promise that the Lord made to the prophet Jeremiah: "Thus saith the LORD; Cursed be the man [or woman] that trusteth in [the things of humanity], and maketh flesh his [or her] arm, and whose heart departeth from the LORD.

"For he [or she] shall be like the . . . desert, and shall not see when good cometh; but shall inhabit the parched places in the wilderness, in a salt land and not inhabited.

"Blessed is the man [and woman] that trusteth in the LORD, and whose hope the LORD is.

"For [they] shall be as a tree planted by the waters, and that spreadeth out her roots by the river, and shall not see when heat cometh, but [their] leaf shall be green; and shall not be careful in the year of drought, neither shall cease from yielding fruit" (Jeremiah 17:5–8).

This can be our promise. We can simultaneously carry on and start over if we will only have faith in the Savior. Let me close by sharing with you President Howard W. Hunter's first *Ensign* First Presidency's message as president of the Church:

He wrote: "Again and again during our Lord's mortal ministry, he issued a call that was at once an invitation and a challenge. . . . 'Follow me.' . . .

"The Lord's invitation to follow him is individual and personal, and . . . compelling. We cannot stand forever between two opinions. Each of us must at some time face the crucial question: 'Whom say ye that I am?' (Matt. 16:15.) Our personal salvation depends on our answer to that question and our commitment to that answer. Peter's revealed answer was 'Thou art the Christ, the Son of the living God' (Matt. 16:16). Many, many witnesses can give an identical answer by the same power, and I join with them in humble gratitude. But we must each answer the question for ourselves—if not now, then later; for at the last day, every knee shall bow and every tongue shall confess that Jesus is the Christ. Our challenge is to answer correctly and live accordingly before it is everlastingly too late. . . .

"Christ's supreme sacrifice can find full fruition in our lives only as we accept the invitation to follow him. This call is not irrelevant, unrealistic, or impossible. To follow an individual means to watch him or listen to him closely; to accept his authority, to take him as a leader, and to obey him; to support and advocate his views; and to take him as a model. Each of us can accept this challenge."[8]

I pray that each of us *will* accept this challenge. I pray that we will simultaneously carry on and start over, that we will build on the strong foundations in our past that represent continuity to us, and that we will joyfully make our new beginnings in areas where change needs to occur.

NOTES

1. Len Walsh, *Read Japanese Today* (Rutland, Vermont, and Tokyo: Charles E. Tuttle Co., 1969), 55.

2. Cesare Pavese, quoted in *Random Acts of Kindness* (Berkeley, California: Conari Press, 1993), 21.

3. As quoted in *Golden Words of Faith, Hope, and Love*, edited by

Louise Bachelder (Mount Vernon, Virginia: Peter Pauper Press, 1969), 10.

4. Ibid., 14.

5. Gordon B. Hinckley, "'It's True, Isn't It?'" *Ensign*, July 1993, 2.

6. *Latter-day Saint Hymns* (Salt Lake City: Deseret Book Co., 1927), no. 377.

7. Quoted in *A Thought for Today*, edited by Theron C. Liddle (Salt Lake City: Deseret News Press, 1961), 19.

8. Howard W. Hunter, "He Invites Us to Follow Him," *Ensign*, September 1994, 2, 4–5.

3

The Wise and the Foolish

When I think about people making commitments, I always think of Elder Vaughn J. Featherstone, who once said that he had always wanted to learn to play the piano. A friend assured him that even though it is not easy to learn and even though Elder Featherstone didn't have much time to practice, if he would work at it for just twenty or thirty minutes a day, he'd be able to play half of the hymns in the hymnbook within five years. Elder Featherstone exclaimed, "Five years! In five years, I'll be sixty-five!"

"Oh?" said the friend. "And how old will you be in five years if you *don't* learn to play the piano?"

I've heard Elder Featherstone tell this story and just laugh and laugh, because of course our time is going to pass, whether we fill it with learning to play the piano or with wishing we had learned to play the piano.

We're all familiar with the story of the wise and foolish virgins, but let's look at it again. According to Jeni and Richard Holzapfel, some modern translations use the words *girls* or *bridesmaids* instead of virgins. And instead of calling them wise or foolish, they use terms such as *clever* or *prudent* or *sensible* vs. *stupid*.[1] But let's use the traditional terms.

"Then shall the kingdom of heaven be likened unto ten

virgins, which took their lamps, and went forth to meet the bridegroom.

"And five of them were wise, and five were foolish.

"They that were foolish took their lamps, and took no oil with them:

"But the wise took oil in their vessels with their lamps.

"While the bridegroom tarried, they all slumbered and slept.

"And at midnight there was a cry made, Behold the bride-groom cometh; go ye out to meet him.

"Then all those virgins arose, and trimmed their lamps."

It helps to know what trimming a lamp means. I grew up in a house without electricity until I was seven, and we used kerosene lamps for light after the sun went down. Even though the lamps were a different shape from those in the Savior's time and kerosene is not the same as olive oil for burning, the idea is the same. When you trim a lamp, you fill it with fuel to the desired level, then you pinch off the burned pieces of the cloth wick so that the ash and dead material won't choke the blaze. Now, back to the story.

"And the foolish said unto the wise, Give us of your oil; for our lamps are gone out.

"But the wise answered, saying, Not so; lest there be not enough for us and you: but go ye rather to them that sell, and buy for yourselves.

"And while they went to buy, the bridegroom came; and they that were ready went in with him to the marriage: and the door was shut.

"Afterward came also the other virgins, saying, Lord, Lord, open to us.

"But he answered and said, Verily I say unto you, I know you not.

"Watch therefore, for ye know neither the day nor the hour wherein the Son of man cometh" (Matthew 25:1–13).

I don't know about you, but there are some troubling parts of this parable to me. For one thing, if I were one of the wise virgins—and I hope I would be but I'm not sure—my impulse, and probably yours as well, would be to share with the foolish virgins when it turned out there was a problem. Isn't that what "charity never faileth" means? As members of the Church, how could we withhold something our brothers and sisters need? Yet this parable makes it plain that the wise virgins are not to share their oil. Why not? That's one of the questions this account raises with me.

The second troubling thing is that when the five foolish virgins return from buying more oil, the door is shut and the bridegroom says, "I know you not." Again, I don't know about you, but this doesn't really sound like Jesus to me, and it doesn't square with my experience of how Jesus treats people.

Sharing Our Preparation

So, as we begin to try to understand this parable, we need to resolve these two troubling questions. Fortunately there are some answers.

President Spencer W. Kimball had strong feelings about this parable and compared the foolish virgins to members of the Church who procrastinate their preparation, neglect their duty, and take lightly their covenants, with the idea that before it grows too late, they will modify their behavior to reflect the things they know to be true. President Kimball observed: "They had the saving, exalting gospel, but it had not been made the center of their lives. They knew the way but gave only a small measure of loyalty and devotion."

When the cry goes out, "The bridegroom cometh," there is no time for preparations that should have already been made. In the parable, the foolish asked the others to share their oil, but President Kimball explains why that is not possible: "This was not selfishness or unkindness. The kind of oil that is needed to illuminate the way and light up the darkness is not shareable. How can one share obedience to the principle of tithing; a mind at peace from righteous living; an accumulation of knowledge? How can one share faith or testimony? How can one share attitudes or chastity, or the experience of a mission? How can one share temple privileges? Each must obtain that kind of oil for [her]self. . . .

"In our lives, the oil of preparedness is accumulated drop by drop in righteous living. Attendance at sacrament meetings adds oil to our lamps, drop by drop over the years. Fasting, family prayer, home teaching, control of bodily appetites, preaching the gospel, studying the scriptures—each act of dedication and obedience is a drop added to our store. Deeds of kindness, payment of offerings and tithes, chaste thoughts and actions, marriage in the covenant for eternity—these, too, contribute importantly to the oil with which we can at midnight refuel our exhausted lamps. . . .

"The day of the marriage feast approaches. The coming of the Lord is nigh. And there are many among us who are not ready for the great and glorious event."[2]

President Kimball's explication of this parable answers my first question: How can we refuse to share when our refusal will keep someone from participating in the great wedding supper of the bridegroom? The answer is that the time to share is now, so that we can prepare together. If attending our meetings adds to our oil drop by drop, then we can encourage our brothers and sisters to attend with us. If we are leaders, we can be sure that a warm and nurturing environment awaits each person, however shy, however uncertain of his or her welcome, however different that person seems to be. If we are teachers, we can be sure that our lessons provide the good bread of the gospel, seasoned with the salt of patience and lavishly spread with the butter and honey of loving kindness, so that all may feast together.

And let's welcome the contributions of others. Let's be sure that the table is large enough so that everyone has a place and welcoming enough that everyone can contribute, whether it's a tuna noodle casserole or an enchilada pie.

An Uncaring Savior?

We could multiply examples of how we can use this time right now to prepare together so that no one—and certainly not 50 percent—will be omitted from the feast of the bridegroom. But let's deal next with the second question that troubled me: Would Jesus Christ, the Son of God, the loving Savior of the world, who allowed himself to be crucified for our sake and who walks the hard and stony paths of mortality beside us, whispering peace into our hearts and upholding us in the hands of his love—would this beloved and loving Savior ever turn away from someone who is seeking to enter his presence?

In the Sermon on the Mount Jesus made a similar, seemingly harsh declaration. Referring to the day of judgment, he said: "By their fruits ye shall know them. Not every one that saith unto me, Lord, Lord, shall enter into the kingdom of heaven; but he that doeth the will of my Father which is in heaven. Many will say to me in that day, Lord, Lord, have we not prophesied in thy name? and in thy name have cast out devils? and in thy name done many wonderful works? And then will I profess unto them, I never knew you: depart from me, ye that work iniquity" (Matthew 7:20–23).

On the surface this appears to be another example of Jesus turning away from people who, apparently sincerely, claim to be his disciples. How can this be?

When Joseph Smith translated the New Testament, one of the passages he corrected was this one. In the Joseph Smith Translation, Jesus says, "And then will I say, Ye never knew me; depart from me ye that work iniquity" (JST Matthew 7:33). Do you hear the difference? The New Testament says, "I never knew you." But the Joseph Smith Translation says, "*Ye* never knew *me.*"

It is not that Jesus or the bridegroom is turning away from someone who sincerely desires to enter his presence; Jesus is saying, with great sorrow but with great honesty, "You claimed to know me. You claimed to be doing my work. You used my name. But you didn't know me." When someone uses the name of Jesus as a cloak for the works he or she does for himself or herself, that person is guilty of a terrible sin. They are taking the name of the Lord in vain. They are committing blasphemy.

We don't talk very much about taking the Lord's name in vain except when we're talking about not swearing or engaging in profanity. But it has this extra meaning as well. As members of the Church, we have taken upon ourselves at the waters of baptism the name of the Savior. In other words, we promise to act as representatives of Christ, to do what he would do if he were present, to say what he would say.

We renew that covenant each week at the sacrament table. Remember what it says? We partake in remembrance of the body or the blood of Jesus Christ and witness to the Father that we are willing to take upon us the name of his Son, promising to always remember him and to keep the commandments he has given us, pleading that if we are obedient we might always have his Spirit to be with us.

It doesn't matter that we come to sacrament meeting every week as imperfect people who have done wrong things for which we are seeking forgiveness. We don't have to be perfect to stretch out our mortal and unclean hands for the small piece of bread and the tiny cup of water. We only need to have a broken heart and a contrite spirit. We only need to be honest with God about what we have done wrong and sincere in our desire to repent and do better. The sacrament isn't for perfect people; it's for imperfect people trying to move in the direction of perfection. It's for us!

That's not the situation I mean when I talk about not taking the Lord's name in vain. We never take his name upon us in vain when we do it with repentant and sincerely loving hearts. In the parable of the ten virgins, the bridegroom, who represents Jesus Christ at the time of the Second Coming, does not turn away from people who sincerely desire to enter his presence. He points out instead that they did not know who he was—that their claims to know him were false and that they had misused his name in covering their lack of charity and responsibility.

Our Personal Power

I want to point out one more lesson from this parable. Jesus tells a whole cluster of parables, one right after the other, to make his point that the Second Coming is a reality but that no one knows when it will be and we have to be prepared at all times. On either side of the parable of the wise and foolish virgins (which involves women) is a parable involving men. The first one is about the unjust steward who is left in charge of the household when the master goes on a journey. At first, the steward is faithful; but when the master delays his coming, the servant becomes corrupt and begins to lord it over the other servants and abuse them. When the master returns, the servant is severely punished for his oppressive ways.

The second parable is that of the talents. When the master leaves, he gives each of three servants a different number of talents (or sums of money). The first two servants are diligent and multiply their talents while the third hides his in the ground. The master is pleased with the first two and rewards them generously, but he punishes the slothful servant who was afraid of him and who chose security rather than working to increase his talent. All of these parables, whether about men or women, have the same message: Be prepared!

I think that the juxtaposition of these parables is no accident. Think of society as it was in Jesus' time. Many of the Jewish customs had their origins in the law of Moses, which was given by God and had deep symbolic significance. But by Jesus' time people no longer remembered or understood the symbolism. As a result of this corruption, women were perceived as second-class citizens and were "generally excluded from public life and were often forced to cover their heads or faces—or both—when in the presence of men. . . . Men, not women, were required to attend regular synagogue worship and the feasts at the temple in Jerusalem." Women were not only considered personally unclean during their menstrual cycle every month but it was thought that they contaminated whatever they touched or sat on. Having sex made the husband ritually unclean afterwards, so couples were forbidden to have intercourse on holy days. Women could not pray in public. They could not wear the prayer shawls and phylacteries or fringes on their garments that were signs of piety and orthodoxy for men. They could not read the scriptures aloud in the synagogue, and some rabbis taught that it was sinful to allow women to read the scriptures at all. Women could not be witnesses in a court of law. Men were forbidden to talk much to women or spend much time with them."[3]

In other words, at the time these parables were given, women were considered incompetent and inferior in every way to men. Yet this parable, while warning women to be prepared for the bridegroom's coming and suggesting that about half of them won't be, is actually a very empowering parable because it makes it so clear that women are responsible for their own spirituality and salvation. There is no suggestion that the fathers or the brothers of these women are responsible for supplying them with oil or that they don't have money to purchase it directly or that they can't make decisions, go to the market, or be out alone at midnight. The message is very clear. We can't wait for someone to do it for us, sisters! And, of course, the message applies equally well to men.

We've explored three lessons from this parable so far. First, the oil that we need for our lamps is acquired by living righteously over many years. It's never too late to start, but it's never too early, either, and the only way we can share our oil with someone else is by encouraging and helping that person to fill his or her own lamp. Second, if our preparation fails and the oil is not accumulated in our hearts where it counts, then even if we claim to be acting in the name of the Lord, he will

say, "Depart from me. You never knew me." We can't be hypocrites. We can't say we're acting for Jesus when we're really
just trying to arrange things for our own advantage.

And the third lesson is that Jesus expects us as women to
prepare ourselves. It's our responsibility and within our power.
It's not our spouse's job or the bishop's job or the Relief
Society president's job. It's yours and it's mine. It's a power
that we each have and it's a responsibility that belongs to
each one of us.

Not Judging

There are two scriptures in the Doctrine and Covenants
that reinforce points made in the parable of the wise and foolish virgins. The first one says that until "the day of the coming
of the Son of Man . . . there will be foolish virgins among the
wise; and at that hour cometh an entire separation of the righteous and the wicked; and in that day will I send mine angels
to pluck out the wicked and cast them into unquenchable fire"
(D&C 63:53–54).

What does this scripture tell us? Does it tell us to figure out
who the foolish virgins are and avoid them at all costs? No, it
says that we will be side by side, the foolish among the wise.
And how will the separation be made at the day of judgment?
Jesus will send his angels to take care of that task.

To me this scripture frees us from the terrible burden of judgment. We don't need to withdraw behind high walls or decide
who can touch us or whom we can serve. We can be together.
We can work together, pray together, and grow together.
Perhaps some whom we think of as foolish and doomed to the
fires of judgment are really among the wise virgins. Perhaps they
are thinking equally negative things about us.

Regarding the judgments we tend to make of others,

Robert L. Millet has written: "It is a sin against charity and a crime against human decency to ignore or belittle or speak unkindly—to judge—those whose children stray. I believe God will hold us accountable if we do so. . . . Maybe there is not much we can do; we probably cannot turn our neighbor's child around on our own. But we can care. We can hurt with our brothers and sisters. And we can pray for them. That's a start. Catchy clichés and platitudes seldom bring comfort, but genuine expressions of love and concern do much to ease the burdens of troubled hearts. . . . We can be forgiving and allow people to change. If Johnny strays from the path for a few years and disqualifies himself for a mission but eventually returns to the path, we can greet him joyfully. God can forgive him, and so must we. If Jennifer leaves the strait and narrow, loses her virtue, has a baby out of wedlock, but chooses eventually to come back to church, we can rejoice in her return. God can forgive her, and so must we. When people have repented, they want desperately to put the past behind them; we as followers of Christ are under covenant to help them do so. In short, if loved ones wander for a time, miss some glorious opportunities and forfeit some blessings, we can still run to meet them while they are yet a great way off (see Luke 15:20)."[4]

How much better, my dear brothers and sisters, to be found waiting and watching for an opportunity to run forward in greeting, like the father of the prodigal son, than to be found, like the Levite and the priest, passing by on the other side of the man wounded on the way to Jericho in the parable of the good Samaritan.

The Spirit As Guide

There is a fifth lesson for us in this parable, and again it is in the words of the modern scriptures that we see an aspect of the parable that was invisible earlier. In Doctrine and Covenants 45:56–59, we read: "And at that day, when I shall come in my glory, shall the parable be fulfilled which I spake concerning the ten virgins. For they that are wise and have received the truth, and have taken the Holy Spirit for their guide, and have not been deceived—verily I say unto you, . . . The earth shall be given unto them for an inheritance; and they shall multiply and wax strong, and their children shall grow up without sin unto salvation. For the Lord shall be in their midst, and his glory shall be upon them, and he will be their king and their lawgiver."

Don't you love that promise? The Lord will be in our midst. The earth will be our inheritance. And our "children shall grow up without sin unto salvation." And in return, what is our task as wise virgins? It is to take the Holy Spirit for our guide that we shall not be deceived.

When I first read this scripture, I was a little startled that it referred to the children of virgins; then I realized that the Lord was broadening its application beyond the parable itself to address the issues directly related to his second coming. The virgins are not unmarried women or even, I would suppose, necessarily women at all, although that interpretation certainly helps us relate to it in this setting. Instead, I think it means those who are innocent—not because they lack experiences in mortality but because they have become guiltless by repenting of their sins and accepting the atonement of Jesus Christ.

Let's focus on our part of this promise: taking the Holy Spirit for our guide and not being deceived. I like to think of the example of a three-legged stool: (1) We need to know what the scriptures say. (2) We need to know what the prophets of our own dispensation say, especially the living prophet. (3) And we need to prayerfully and earnestly seek the guidance of the Holy Ghost. The scriptures were not necessarily written as personal counsel to us, even though a passage will often speak to us with such force and freshness that it seems as if it were made just for us. The Holy Spirit is the messenger from Heavenly Father, who knows our individual needs and circumstances in intimate detail and who will guide us individually in the paths we are to follow.

Here are three stories that show how the Spirit guides us in a world that God loves and touches and pays attention to:

"When a team of Christians visited Savropol, Russia, in 1994 to hand out Bibles, a local citizen said he recalled seeing Bibles in an old warehouse. They had been confiscated in the 1930s when Stalin was sending believers to the gulags. Amazingly, the Bibles were still there.

"Among those who showed up to load them into trucks was a young agnostic student just wanting to earn a day's wage. But soon he slipped away from the job. . . . A team member went looking for him and found him sitting in a corner weeping. Out of the hundreds of Bibles, he had picked up one that bore the handwritten signature of his own grandmother. Persecuted for her faith, she had no doubt prayed often for her family and her city. God used that grandmother's Bible to [touch] that young man."[5]

How could this woman have known or guessed that God would put her Bible into the hands of her own struggling grandchild? The answer is, she couldn't, but because she did not renounce her faith as a Christian, her Bible and her grandson were brought together sixty years later when the time was right.

That's a pretty spectacular example of the miracle of being led by the Spirit. Here's a much smaller example told by Luci Swindoll, a Christian woman who with a friend named Marilyn was trying to find an address in Riverside, California. They weren't Mormons, but if they had been, they would have been visiting teaching companions, so think of them that way:

"[I] . . . was navigating with a map of the area as we diligently searched for a short little street named 'Iowa.' The map wasn't very helpful, actually. Only the major streets were clearly delineated. Finally, after turning the map to the right and left, even upside down, I finally saw in fine print a tiny street called IOWA.

"'Turn off on Columbia, Mar[ilyn],' I advised, 'then make an immediate right. . . .' Marilyn did exactly as I said, [but] after driving for several blocks, still there was no 'Iowa.'

" . . . We started back the other way. While we waited for a red light to change and pondered where on earth this little street could be, a UPS truck pulled up on our left and a beat-up pickup truck came up on our right. The guy in the pickup yelled through our open windows to the guy in the UPS truck: 'Yo, where's Iowa?'

"Without the slightest hesitation, the UPS guy yelled back, 'Up the street two blocks and to the left. Can't miss it.' We could hardly believe it. . . . We received perfect instructions from two total strangers as they conversed through our car. [We] . . . found Iowa right where it was supposed to be."[6]

Here is one last story from my own Japanese heritage. Perhaps you have seen the movie *Schindler's List*, which dramatizes how a Polish businessman, who was not very moral but whose heart was touched by the plight of the Jews, rescued many from the concentration camps by putting them to work in his factories. But you may not have heard about Chiune Sugihara, a Japanese diplomat who was stationed in Lithuania in 1939. He "saved thousands of Polish Jews from the Nazis by issuing transit visas to them. Defying his own government, he wrote visas day and night, even scribbling them by hand and passing them through a train window as he departed [from] Lithuania."

He was almost forgotten after the war; but survivors started to tell his story, and he came to the attention of the Israeli government who wanted to honor "courageous rescuers," such as Sugihara.

"One of the ways the Jewish state attempted to acknowledge its debt was by . . . planting trees in their honor. When Sugihara's valor came to light, Israeli officials immediately made plans to plant a cherry grove, as was customary, in his memory. But suddenly, in an uncommon move, officials . . . opted instead for a grove of cedar trees, deciding that cedar was sturdier and had holier connotations, having been used in the First Temple.

"It was only after they had planted the trees that the astonished officials learned for the first time that 'Sugihara' in Japanese means . . . cedar grove."[7]

Now, this wasn't a miracle that made a difference either to Chiune Sugihara, who was dead, or to the State of Israel. But what it does is communicate to everyone who hears this story that God had not turned away from even the terrible moment in human history known as the Holocaust. For me, this story, which could be explained as an odd coincidence, communicates that God is everywhere.

And what about the other two stories? Well, Iowa isn't in the scriptures and the prophet has yet to be in Russia. But God knew where Iowa Street was and figured out a way to get that information to Luci and Marilyn, and the Spirit that strengthened that Russian grandmother even while her Bible was being confiscated by ruthless Stalinists knew that there would be a season of joy as that dead grandmother laid her hand in living testimony on the agnostic heart of her grandson and made him a believer. Truly the Lord is in our midst. When we live in the Spirit, he is our king and our lawgiver.

Conclusion

Remember the five lessons from this parable about the wise and foolish virgins. First, the oil of preparation we have in our lamps is acquired by living righteously over many years. We can't give someone our testimony of the temple, but we can help that person develop his or her own testimony.

Second, if Jesus turns away from us at the last day, it will not be because he doesn't love us but because we have been hypocrites in our lives: it will be because we have claimed to know him and love him and act in his name, but have not done his work. Instead we have tried to benefit ourselves by claiming the Lord's authority to intimidate or manipulate others.

The third lesson is that Jesus expects us to take responsibility for ourselves and not wait for our spouse or anyone else to tell us what to do.

The fourth lesson is that Jesus will send his angels to separate the wise from the foolish, the wheat from the tares, in the last day. So we don't have to judge. We don't have to condemn. We don't have to hold ourselves aloof from people whom we think are foolish.

And the fifth lesson, the promise to those who are wise in this life, is that we will be guided by the Holy Spirit; and by following it, we will have steadfastness and peace. We will see our children "grow up without sin unto salvation."

May we be among the wise and not among the foolish. May we help each other to be wise, to be loving, to know Jesus and to be known by him.

NOTES

1. Jeni Broberg Holzapfel and Richard Neitzel Holzapfel, *Sisters at the Well: Women and the Life and Teachings of Jesus* (Salt Lake City: Bookcraft, 1993), 71.

2. Spencer W. Kimball, *Faith Precedes the Miracle* (Salt Lake City: Deseret Book Co., 1977), 253–57.

3. Holzapfel and Holzapfel, *Women at the Well*, 17–18.

4. Robert L. Millet, *When a Child Wanders* (Salt Lake City: Deseret Book, 1996), 45–47.

5. Dennis J. De Haan, "For Future Generations," in *Our Daily Bread* (Grand Rapids, Michigan: RBC Ministries, 1996), 8.

6. Luci Swindoll, "Where's Iowa?" in *Joy Breaks* (Grand Rapids, Michigan: Zondervan Publishing House, 1997), 199.

7. Yitta Halberstam and Judith Leventhal, *Small Miracles* (Holbrook, Massachussetts: Adams Media Corporation, 1997), 132–33.

4

A PERFECT BRIGHTNESS OF HOPE

---　✦　---

e have been promised eternal life—but only on certain conditions: "Wherefore, ye must press forward with a steadfastness in Christ, having a perfect brightness of hope, and a love of God and of all men [and women]. Wherefore, if ye shall press forward, feasting upon the word of Christ, and endure to the end, behold, thus saith the Father: Ye shall have eternal life" (2 Nephi 31:20).

This is such a richly packed scripture! There are so many concepts within it that it is hard to select just one to concentrate on. Let's look at these concepts: First comes the necessity of pressing forward. Second, we need to possess four qualities: steadfastness in Christ, a perfect brightness of hope, a love of God, and a love of all men and women. Third, to help us press forward, we must feast on the word of Christ. Fourth, we must endure to the end. These are the things we must do; and in exchange, the Father promises us, "Ye shall have eternal life." This verse establishes a covenant. If we promise to do certain things that only we can do, the Father in turn promises to give us something that is within only his power to grant us.

I'd like to concentrate on one of these concepts—having a brightness of hope. And I'd like to present it this way so it's easier to remember: We know *who* we are when we know *whose* we are. If we look strictly at our own uneven track records, most of us might feel that we have hope but not a very bright hope. Well, my message to you is the same hope that Nephi gives his people in the verse above. Our hope is not in our own strength but in the strength of Christ, "who is mighty to save." We are assured that we can have "unshaken faith" in him and rely "wholly" on his ability to make up our deficiencies (see 2 Nephi 31:19).

We sometimes get a lot of negative messages about what will happen if we sin. It's very easy to end up feeling guilty and ashamed and like failures because, let's face it, we *are* guilty and sinful. We do fail. We really do do things we're ashamed of. And the scriptures point out this dark side. But sometimes we concentrate on the dark side instead of on the bright side. For instance, Paul compares the body to a temple, then goes on to say, "If any man defile the temple of God, him shall God destroy" (1 Corinthians 3:17). This scripture gets used a lot to warn us about the dangers of having illicit sex and using drugs and violating the Word of Wisdom.

Such warnings are certainly appropriate, but I'd like to skip the warnings for the moment, and instead present a whole string of promises. The reason for doing this is that I don't meet very many Latter-day Saints who need much convincing that they're sinful and need a Savior. I do meet a lot of Latter-day Saints who, because they feel so awful about themselves, need some convincing that they're worth saving.

The fact is, Jesus knows all about us. He knows everything we do. He's heard every word we've whispered under our breath. He knows what we think about in the dark hours after midnight. And guess what! He is not shocked. He is not disgusted. He is not repulsed. He loves us. He reaches out to us. He is beside us, lifting us into his everlasting arms. When we think about being the temple of God we need to remember that he also says that we are temples of "the Holy Ghost . . . , which ye have of God, and ye are not your own[.] For ye are bought with a price: therefore glorify God in your body, and in your spirit, which are God's" (1 Corinthians 6:19–20).

He has promised us, "I will never leave thee, nor forsake thee. So that we may boldly say, The Lord is my helper, and I will not fear what [anyone] shall do unto me" (Hebrews 13:5–6).

Consider God's additional assurances of his love and our potential: "And they who keep their first estate shall be added upon; . . . and they who keep their second estate shall have glory added upon their heads for ever and ever" (Abraham 3:26).

"The Spirit itself beareth witness with our spirit, that we are the children of God: And if children, then heirs; heirs of God, and joint-heirs with Christ; if so be that we suffer with him, that we may be also glorified together" (Romans 8:16–17).

"Fear not, little children, for you are mine, and I have overcome the world, and you are of them that my Father hath given me; and none of them that my Father hath given me shall be lost" (D&C 50:41–42).

"And he that receiveth my Father receiveth my Father's kingdom; therefore all that my Father hath shall be given unto him" (D&C 84:38).

"And as I said unto mine apostles, even so I say unto you, . . . ye are they whom my Father hath given me; ye are my friends" (D&C 84:63).

So if you're feeling too discouraged or evil or ashamed to approach Christ, if you're feeling downcast and hopeless, those feelings are not coming from Jesus. Don't think that you have to suffer and grovel and beat yourself up after making a mistake before you can approach Jesus for help. Don't think you have to weep and wail for a certain number of hours to attract his attention or impress him with your contrition. He knows your heart. He knows whether you're sincerely sorry or not. He doesn't say, "Go to your room" or "Go directly to jail without passing GO." He says, "Come unto me."

Come to him, my dear brothers and sisters. Make haste! Don't let even a second pass between recognizing that you've done something you're ashamed of and turning instantly to Jesus to beg forgiveness and ask for strength.

Who would be so stupid as to break a leg rock-climbing and then, to teach your leg a lesson, walk around on it for a week without having it set? Obviously that wouldn't teach your leg a lesson. It would just make it harder to heal. In the same way, don't try to teach yourself a lesson by wallowing in your guilt and embarrassment and shame after you've done something wrong. Let that first flicker of shame be a signal to you that not only have you done something wrong but that you must instantly turn to Jesus, confess your fault, beg his forgiveness, and then make what amends you can. Don't let your shame become a space separating you from Jesus, a space in which dark thoughts and even darker deeds can grow.

Now, let's explore the concept of having a perfect brightness of hope in Christ and, as a result, having a realistic hope in our own capabilities, in our ability to develop our faith and increase our righteousness. Our heavenly parents didn't send us here to be a secondhand anything, and Jesus didn't die for us because we were such pathetic wimps that somebody had to take mercy on us. He died for us because we are eternal beings, his spiritual brothers and sisters, capable of enlargement, with unlimited potential. Faith in Christ and a perfect brightness of hope in him is our inalienable legacy as children of God, a son or daughter of Christ, a joint-heir with Christ of all the Father has.

Developing Self-Esteem

In my view, self-esteem exists when we know where we fit in the eternal scheme of things—when we know who we are and whose we are. Now, there are a lot of things that can erode or damage our self-esteem if we were to let them. I want to tell you about a truly heroic role model along these lines—Elder Spencer J. Condie. He talks about twice being mistaken for President Gordon B. Hinckley. The first time, he corrected the person, but felt so sorry at her chagrin that he didn't correct the second. When he related this experience to President Hinckley, President Hinckley said, with his typical humor: "Well, Spencer, if you're going to impersonate me, I hope you behave yourself."[1]

This wasn't the only problem Elder Condie had encountered.

"When I was in my teens I sometimes helped my mother scrub the kitchen floor. One Saturday morning as we were on our knees together, Mother, well known for her candor, said: 'Son, you're now old enough to know—you're not very good-looking. I don't want you to go through high school conceited and thinking you're the answer to every girl's prayers.'"

How would a message like that from your mother make you feel? "Well, thanks a lot, Mom! You could have gone my whole lifetime without sharing that particular insight!" Brother Condie says:

"Well, I knew my mother loved me, so I shrugged off her observation without too much lingering damage to my self-esteem. I went on a mission, graduated from college, got married, and was much relieved that a wife so beautiful would even consider being seen with me in public.

"Following graduate school I joined the faculty of Brigham Young University, and shortly thereafter a friend from high school days, who was working for the BYU Motion Picture Studio, called to invite me to be involved in a filmstrip they were producing on time management. Always wanting to be helpful, I cheerfully acceded to his request and showed up at the studio for a recording and photography session. I was to play the role of an extremely busy young bishop, and one of my lines was: 'There are so many things I have to do, I just can't seem to find the time to get them all done.' They recorded my lines several times to assure they had a good recording, and then they told me thanks and said good-bye.

"I asked, 'But when do we do the photography?'

"The producer of the filmstrip indicated that the photography takes place separately, a few weeks after they have edited the audio recordings.

"I returned to my office and waited for the phone to ring informing me that I was to return to the studio to be photographed in various scenes accompanying the recorded script. The phone call never came.

"Some time later I was invited to a large meeting of Saints where it was explained that a recently produced filmstrip on time management would be shown. Sure enough, here was the premiere showing of the filmstrip in which I had participated. As the filmstrip progressed, we observed a tall, dark, and handsome bishop who said, in a voice very familiar to me: 'There are so many things I have to do, I just can't seem to find the time to get them all done.' I thought to myself: *Those unscrupulous knaves agree with my mother—they'll use my voice, but not my face.*"[2]

If you have ever had hurt feelings because you have been overlooked or because your contribution has been slighted, you will do well to remember Elder Condie. If he had been counting on others to bolster his self-esteem or to make him feel valued, he would have been staggering long before President Hinckley counseled him to behave himself while "impersonating" him. Instead, he made his experience one we can all share in good humor, even if we're saying, "Ouch!" at the same time. And it's a wonderful reminder that self-esteem comes from the inside, not from the outside.

Decide Who You Are

To develop a perfect brightness of hope, it is also important to decide who you are. I like the way Julia Cameron defined herself: "I am a particle and an article of faith."[3] How do you define yourself? Do you have a particle of faith in the glorious promises made by our Lord Jesus Christ? Is your life an article of faith? Does faith in who you are and whose you are illuminate your actions, radiate in your words, and find physical embodiment in your actions? If the answer is "yes," or even "Yes, most of the time," then you don't have any concerns about self-esteem that you and the Savior can't handle together in your daily prayers.

If you know who you are, it makes it simpler to make goals for yourself and work toward them. If you know who you are, your commitments and covenants are more profoundly meaningful. Knowing who you are makes it easier to deal with discordant information and disappointments. And I'll tell you something else: If you know who you are and how you want to be treated, then it makes it much easier for other people to meet your needs and to do it joyfully and graciously. In his book *All I Really Need to Know I Learned in Kindergarten*, Robert Fulghum tells a wonderful story that illustrates this point.

In an effort to entertain and manage a group of eighty rambunctious schoolchildren, Fulghum devised a game of "Giants, Wizards, and Dwarfs." The game would provide the children a way to run off excess energy but also require them to make some decisions. At one point in the game, Fulghum announced to the wired-up competitors, "You have to decide now which you are—a GIANT, a WIZARD, or a DWARF!

"As they quickly huddled in frenzied, whispered consultation, a small girl tugged on Fulghum's pant leg. 'Where do the Mermaids stand?' she asked.

" 'Where do the Mermaids stand?' says I.

" 'Yes. You see, I am a Mermaid.'

" 'There are no such things as Mermaids.'

" 'Oh, yes, I am one!'

"The little girl did not relate to being a Giant, a Wizard, or a Dwarf. But she was not to be excluded. She just assumed there was a place for her and demanded that she be shown."[4]

It's not hard to understand the point of this story. This little girl who was the mermaid knew who she was and could claim a place, even though at the moment it seemed that there was no place for her. If you feel excluded, claim your place, even if you have to make a place. Participate. Understand what that place is and be happy in it.

In most Mormon gatherings, if I were to ask who you are, particularly what your eternal identity is, many would answer,

"I am a child of God." It's a beautiful answer, shaped by the Primary song we have known and learned and loved for two generations. But that is not enough. Every living person is a child of God. But that's the beginning point, not the ending point. The ending point is to become peers of God, friends of God, coworkers with God, adults of God. He wants us to grow up, not remain children.

I think that some of us sometimes regress to being two-year-olds of God and have tantrums when things don't go our way or when we get tired or scared. Some of us get stuck being teenagers of God, who just got a driver's license and are out to see how fast we can move our lives from one lane to the next and play some pretty reckless and heedless games with this precious life God has given us. Some of us jump ahead and are Alzheimer's patients of God where our short-term memory is disappearing and we keep repeating the same mistakes over and over again because we can't remember that the exact same thing we're doing right now didn't work before either. Some of us are junkies of God and go from one spiritual book or speaker or Education Week to another without ever thoughtfully sifting and sorting and laying out the pieces of our lives before God and asking him to help us shape these pieces into something meaningful. Some of us are workaholics of God. We plunge into our callings and our service projects and our personal gospel study and our genealogical research and God becomes somebody we meet at the drinking fountain or the copy machine long enough to gasp out a quick report before we rush off to the next project.

Well, I hope that somewhere in your personal definition of who you are that there are descriptions such as "lover of God" and "disciple of Christ" and "handmaiden of the Lord" and "servant of the Most High" and even the term that Christ himself used: "friend" of God.

Living Richly

I'd like to suggest something very concrete that you can do to make yourself more aware of how intensely our Heavenly Father and the Savior love you, and that's to live with gratitude. A man named Wilferd Peterson, about whom I know nothing but whose thought I greatly admire, wrote indirectly about this topic when he suggested that we all find ways to "live richly," then explained what he meant:

> The art of becoming rich is simply to live richly in body, mind, heart, and spirit.
>
> You become physically rich when you have rich sensations: When your senses are alert and attuned to life so that the very fact of being alive takes on new dimensions and simple experiences have new meaning. . . . The smell of a rose, the stretch of a muscle, the sight of a mountain, the sound of the surf, the taste of strawberries, the touch of clean white sheets . . .
>
> You become mentally rich when you think rich thoughts: When you immerse your mind in the noble thoughts of [others], preserved through the ages in books; when you are curious to learn all you can about the world and its people, the earth beneath your feet and the farthest star in infinite space; when you develop an appreciation of beauty in painting and sculpture, poetry and music; when you expand your mind to encompass great ideas; when you use the magic of your mind to create and to serve. . . .
>
> You become emotionally rich when you have rich

feelings: When you know the radiant glow of obeying noble impulses to give and help and inspire; when you experience the bond of warm friendship and deep affection; when you know the joy of hearing a baby laugh; when you are aware of giving and receiving love. . . .

You become spiritually rich when you discover the riches of the kingdom within: When you have a consciousness of the oneness of all life; when you experience kinship with nature; when you are open to the buoyant spiritual life of being in tune with the Infinite; when you know the power of meditation and prayer.

The best definition of a rich man [or woman] is a [person] with a rich self. What a [person] is, not what he [or she] has, is the measure of real wealth.[5]

And I would suggest that developing a keen awareness of the kind of riches Wilferd Peterson is talking about will deepen and broaden our sense of gratitude to God for the abundance of blessings in which we live and move. Feeling this kind of gratitude, and feeling immersed and drenched in blessings, is a wonderful corrective to feeling discouraged about ourselves or sorry for ourselves. On the contrary, we know exactly where we fit in a pattern that is larger than we are.

The reason this technique of living richly is so powerful is that it keeps in our own control all of the forces necessary for inner peace and contentment. I don't know that Wilferd Peterson thought of Abraham Lincoln while writing about the concept of living richly, but Lincoln certainly came to my mind. Lincoln once said, "I have found that when one is embarrassed, usually the shortest way to get through with it is to quit talking about it or thinking about it, and go at something else."[6] Remember what I said about not wallowing in guilt and grief? Here we are approaching the same idea from a different direction. One of Lincoln's biographers has noted:

"Lincoln certainly had his share of unhappy experiences. Often, they plunged him into depression so severe that his friends feared for him. Gradually, though, he discovered what to do when he was rejected, belittled, or attacked. He taught himself to view failures as experiences to learn from instead of disasters to be brooded over. He learned when to stop worrying and move on to something else.

"Perhaps most important was Lincoln's growing ability to validate himself. He had no desperate need for others' praise to be self-confident. That knowledge came from within."[7]

Knowing who we are and liking who we are means that we take our own capacity for failure calmly. Living richly means that we don't minimize the pain of mistakes or lie to ourselves about them. It means that we keep them in perspective and learn from them. But above all, it means that we do not contaminate the sources of our self-esteem by confusing who we are with what we do. As long as we're human, we will make mistakes. Count on it. Get used to it. And get over it.

Don't, for mercy's sake, believe that Jesus loves you because you're so lovable. He loves you because he's so loving! You can't buy his love, beg his love, borrow his love, blackmail his love, steal his love, or bargain for his love. You already have it: measured out, pressed down, shaken together, and running over.

Rabbi Kushner says: "A lot of misery could be traced to this one mistaken notion [that] we need to be perfect for people to love us and we forfeit that love if we ever fall short of perfection. There are few emotions more capable of leaving us feeling bad about ourselves than the conviction that we don't deserve to be loved, and few ways more certain to generate that conviction than the idea that every time we do something wrong, we give God and the people closest to us reasons not to love us."[8]

I think this is what the Apostle Paul was trying to communicate when he told the Ephesian Saints that some were "able to do exceeding abundantly above all that we ask or think." Why? "According to the power that worketh in us" (Ephesians 3:20). In other words, we don't have to do it on our own. Paul returned to this theme when he wrote to the Philippian Saints: "For it is God which worketh in you both to will and to do of his good pleasure" (Philippians 2:13).

Could anything be clearer? God isn't standing by with a stopwatch in his hand saying, "Well, Jenny, you're not running as fast as Lisa. I'm so disappointed in you." Or "Eric, you stumbled coming around that corner on your last lap. One more time and I'm throwing you out of the race!" No, he's running with us. He's pacing us, encouraging us, even giving us a helping hand. We are not competing with God or with each other for our salvation.

I was looking at my mission diary a little while ago. My husband, Ed, and I were called to the Japan Okinawa Mission in 1968, a brand-new mission that had just been split off from an existing mission. We had to learn everything from scratch. We were both converts. We'd never served missions. Of course we wanted to do our very best, but we didn't always know the best thing to do, even after we fasted and prayed and studied hard. What if we'd been paralyzed by our own mistakes? What if we felt hopeless every time we made a mistake? And we made a lot!

It helped me to realize that I wouldn't think of getting angry with the members or the missionaries when they didn't understand something or when they made a mistake. I was just so grateful that they were trying. I recorded in my diary an experience I had in a Relief Society homemaking meeting when I tried to teach the sisters how to bake an American-style cake. Now, you may ask why we even thought this was important to do. Here I was, a Japanese-American woman from Hawaii, teaching Japanese women without ovens how to make and frost cakes. Couldn't we have concentrated on Japanese-style specialties? Well, yes, we could have, but the sisters were really delighted to learn American-style cooking because of the popularity of American things. In fact, one of our most successful Christmas activities for the neighborhood was making popcorn balls. We had people standing in line trying to figure out how popcorn worked and then trying to mold the sticky concoction into balls. But back to the cakes. My diary for 3 December 1970 reads:

"Went to Abeno Relief Society at 1:00 P.M. and taught the sisters how to make cake. We had lots of fun. It was interesting to watch these sisters. One would wonder if a cake would ever turn out from the way they were making them. But because of [the] bad oven, some of them got burnt on the bottom, but the taste and texture was good. They are so eager to learn. Made the chocolate frosting which they used to cover the bad part of the cake. They were happy over what took place. . . . Fun to see Honda Shimai and Tsuyama Shimai making the white frosting and then see that they put in so much cornstarch that it turned out so hard. Well, it was fun!"

And this is the point! I was so happy to be with these sisters, sharing my knowledge and encouraging them to try new things. My hope was that the woman who was willing to try making a cake, even in an oven with an uncontrollable temperature that would burn the bottom, would next be willing to try something more difficult, such as praying in public, because she had learned that it was okay to make mistakes.

Conclusion

I bear testimony that we can have a brightness of hope, not because we are so good at polishing up our hope-reflectors but because the source of that hope is so bright. Our hope is in Jesus Christ, and he will never fail us.

Remember Elder Condie and the many messages he received that could have damaged his self-esteem? Decide who you are. Be a particle and an article of faith. Be a mermaid. Be an adult of God. Be a friend of God.

And then do. Live richly and gratefully. Take mistakes in stride. Don't let them cripple you. Take the work we are engaged in seriously. Take your relationship with Christ and with each other seriously.

Remember the assurances of Christ's love and the promises of his everlasting interest in us, which were cited at the beginning of this chapter. I know that we do not know even a hint of the abundance and plenty and riches that await us as we open our hearts to the boundless love of Christ—not only in the mansions of eternity but in this glorious and bewildering plethora of choices and opportunities right here, right now, before us today. Let us take Christ at his word and trust his love and open our hearts to give and receive even more love.

NOTES

1. Spencer J. Condie, "A Mighty Change of Heart," *Ensign*, November 1993, 15.

2. Spencer J. Condie, *Your Agency: Handle with Care* (Salt Lake City: Bookcraft, 1996), 28–30.

3. Julia Cameron, *Heart Steps* (New York: Jeremy P. Tarcher/ Putnam, 1997), 3.

4. Robert Fulghum, *All I Really Need to Know I Learned in Kindergarten* (New York: Ivy Books, 1986), 81–83.

5. Wilferd A. Peterson, *More about the Art of Living* (New York, New York: Simon and Schuster, 1966), 16–17.

6. Gene Griessman, *The Words Lincoln Lived By* (New York: Fireside, 1997), 40.

7. Ibid., 41.

8. Harold S. Kushner, *How Good Do We Have to Be?* (Boston, Massachussetts: Little, Brown and Company, 1996), 9.

5

LISTENING TO THE SPIRIT

he Savior promises each of us: "Learn of me, and listen to my words; walk in the meekness of my Spirit, and you shall have peace in me" (D&C 19:23). Listening to the Spirit is a powerful and empowering concept. It frees us from the overwhelming amount of meaningless chatter and conflicting messages that flood our worlds. Learning how to listen is an empowering skill.

I'm not going to spend any time on things we all know about how to *prepare* to listen to the Spirit—things such as keeping the commandments, serving in the temple, following the prophet, studying the scriptures, and fulfilling our callings. All of us already understand these things. Instead, I'd like to focus on three concepts related to listening to the Spirit. The first is that we have to choose to listen. The second is that listening to the Spirit will allow us to face the future with faith. And the third is that following the Spirit will help us find contentment in the present—in each day of our daily lives.

Choosing to Listen

I recently visited my grandsons in Colorado, and one of the things we did was to color and draw together. Now, you may not know—I didn't—that Binney & Smith, the people who make Crayola crayons, announced eight new colors to celebrate the company's anniversary. To mark the occasion, they also publicized some little-known facts about crayons: the average child in the United States will wear down 730 crayons by the time he or she is ten. The company turns out an average of 5 million crayons a day, or more than two billion each year. Although there are 104 colors (including the eight new ones), the labels are made in only eighteen colors. And the box of twenty-four crayons is the company's best-seller.[1]

If you can remember back that far, you probably had a favorite Crayola color when you were a child. I got to prolong my childhood by teaching grade school for twenty-three years and then being a principal for another ten, and I was frequently invited to sit down and color or draw with the class I was visiting.

I've worn down lots more than my share of 730 crayons, but my favorite color has always been red. I'm not sure why, but it's a color that is bright, alive, and strong. I looked for red everywhere and found it: in the sunsets, in the fire, when the lobsters turned red. It was a color that my mother loved, too; and since she made most of my clothes, she often dressed me in red. I remember wearing red when I learned Japanese dances.

Now my grandson Andrew happens to like blue, so all of his blue crayons—sky blue, pale blue, royal blue, navy blue—were worn down to nubbins. And the favorite color of his older brother, Matthew, is green.

But the important point is that we all choose our favorite colors. Nobody tells us what we have to choose. What is the role of choice in listening to the Spirit and in shaping our attitude toward our future and our present?

Janet G. Lee told a very poignant story about her five-year-old daughter, Stephanie. She wrote:

I took her to register for kindergarten. When we arrived, she was invited to go into a classroom to "play games" with the teachers and other children. As a former elementary school teacher, I was certain that the "games" were a method of testing for placement purposes.

A teacher was sitting just outside the room with a box of crayons and several sheets of blank paper; and I smiled confidently to myself from across the hall as Stephanie was asked to choose her favorite color and write her name. "She could write *all* the names in our family," I thought to myself. "She is so well prepared, there isn't anything in that room she can't handle." But Stephanie just stood there. The teacher repeated the instructions, and again my daughter stood still, staring blankly at the box of crayons, with her knees locked and her hands behind her back.

In the sweet, patient voice that teachers use when they are beginning to feel slightly *impatient*, the teacher asked once more, "Stephanie, choose your favorite color, dear, and write your name on this paper." I was about to come to my daughter's aid when the teacher kindly said, "That's okay. We will help you learn to write your name when you come to school in the fall." With all the restraint I could gather, I watched Stephanie move into the classroom with a teacher who believed [that] my daughter did not know how to write her name.

On the way home, I tried to ask as nonchalantly as

possible why she had not written her name. "I couldn't," she replied. "The teacher said to choose my favorite color, and there wasn't a pink crayon in the box!"[2]

Sister Lee commented, "How many times are we, as Heavenly Father's children, immobilized because the choice we had in mind for ourselves just isn't available to us, at least not at the time we want it?

"Is progress halted when acceptance into a chosen major is denied, when enrollment in a required class is closed, when a desired job doesn't come through, when that dream date doesn't progress beyond friendship, or when the money hoped for isn't there? Are we ever, for reasons that are hard to understand or beyond our control, faced with a set of circumstances that we did not have in mind for ourselves? In other words, what happens when we look in the box, and the pink crayon just isn't there?"[3]

Sister Lee's point is a good one. But I also see a different meaning in it. Stephanie at age five may not have understood that she had some options. One of those options was to say, "My favorite crayon is pink. Will you please find me a pink crayon?" Another option was to say, "I don't see my favorite crayon there, but I see my next-favorite crayon. May I use that?" In other words, Stephanie could have asked some questions about the experience that was being presented to her.

Sometimes we tend not to ask questions about options because we feel that we need to think, believe, and act the same way as everyone else. There are different ways we can react. We can choose to be passive or active, to ask questions or be silent, conform to social pressure or resist the status quo. I think we need to make more active choices more of the time.

The point I'm making about listening to the Spirit is this. We sometimes think that the hard part of listening to the Spirit is to persuade the Spirit to talk to us. That's absolutely not true. The Spirit is on call and fully available twenty-four hours a day. It whispers continuously as the "still small voice, which whispereth through and pierceth all things" (D&C 85:6). It's a persistent voice. It is always available either for a direct question or a thorough, open-ended exploration. But because it is both still and small, it can be drowned out by the hiss and buzz and static of our hurried, distracted lives. The problem isn't that the Spirit isn't talking. The problem is that we aren't listening.

This is why I make the point about choosing. The Spirit is always speaking, but we must choose to listen. The Savior promises that "the Holy Ghost shall be thy constant companion, and thy scepter an unchanging scepter of righteousness and truth" (D&C 121:46). But this isn't the same thing as saying that we're the Holy Ghost's constant companion, is it? We must choose to notice who our companions are. This isn't mysterious or complicated or hard. Would you notice the absence of your three-year-old? Would you notice if your teenager isn't in the house when you wake up in the morning? Would you notice if the secretary isn't in the office or if your spouse isn't present at the supper table? Of course you would.

In the same way, noticing the presence of the Spirit begins with the fervent prayer uttered many times each day, "Please let the Spirit be with me." This prayer is coupled with the equally short, equally fervent prayer of thanksgiving when you feel the Spirit's presence. Nephi rebuked his brothers because they were "slow to remember" and because they didn't pay attention to the feelings that the Spirit roused in them until "[they] were past feeling, [and] could not feel his words" (1 Nephi 17:45). The message to us is to pay attention to those feelings and to be quick to remember.

You *know*—you just plain *know*—where the Spirit is, the same way that you know your three-year-old is finishing her breakfast or has gone back to the bedroom to look for her shoe.

Paul tells the Ephesians not to "grieve . . . the holy Spirit of God" and warns them to avoid the "bitterness, and wrath, and anger, and clamour, and evil speaking" that will deprive them of his sweet companionship (Ephesians 4:30–31). It's true that there are places that the Spirit can't go with us. It can't go into anger or spitefulness or the desire to hurt. It can't be present when you're gossiping or punishing or whining. But you don't really want it there, either, any more than you'd want to take your teenager into a bar. So giving up these nasty little pleasures is no loss at all.

Choose the Spirit. Choose to listen. I promise you, you will hear and understand and love his voice.

Faith in the Future

Think about the difference this constant companionship makes to our hurried, worried, often frightening futures. Think of the Apostle Paul at the time he wrote four beautiful epistles, those to the Ephesians, Philippians, Colossians, and to Philemon. These letters "are among the most hopeful and encouraging Paul wrote. They help us understand how we can find joy in our trials and peace in our suffering."[4] We know from what Paul says that he was in chains and guarded. At some points, he was even chained *to* the guard. Yet, the message to the Philippians contains the word *joy* or one of its variants sixteen times.

Let's look at this more closely. Philippians is a short letter, only four chapters long, and it contains a total of 104 verses: Paul tells the Saints that he "always in every prayer of mine for you" asks "with joy" that they will retain their testimonies of the gospel (1:4). He assures them that his faith is strong and that he rejoices in his captivity, "yea, and will rejoice. For I know that this shall turn to my salvation" (1:18–19). If he dies, he will be with the Savior; if he lives, he will be able to bring more people to a knowledge of the truth. He speaks of the "joy of faith" (1:25) and sounds only a little wistful thinking of the "more abundant . . . rejoicing" (1:26) he would feel if he could see the Philippian Saints again. "Fulfil ye my joy," he urges them, by "having the same love, being of one accord, of one mind" (2:2). Paul prays that he "may rejoice in the day of Christ" in their faithfulness (2:16). "I joy, and rejoice with you all. For the same cause also do ye joy, and rejoice with me" (2:17–18). He is sending this message by Epaphroditus, "that . . . ye may rejoice . . . Receive him therefore in the Lord with all gladness" (2:28–29).

Paul, in bearing his testimony of the resurrection, writes what amounts to a hymn of praise to the Lord, the chorus of which is rejoicing: "Rejoice in the Lord" (3:1), "rejoice in Christ Jesus" (3:3), "my brethren [and sisters] dearly beloved and longed for, my joy and crown," (4:1), "Rejoice in the Lord alway: and again I say, Rejoice" (4:4). "I [rejoice] in the Lord greatly" (4:10).

Isn't this remarkable? He is in prison, no doubt under very uncomfortable circumstances, chained up and cooped up when he has been used to plying the Mediterranean Sea and striding full speed down the roads of Asia Minor, under threat of death and, indeed, fully facing the fact that he may soon die and may never see his loved ones, including the Philippians, again. How is this attitude of rejoicing possible? And what lessons can he teach us about how we should contemplate our future and deal with our present?

First, I think it is very important that he does not condition his future happiness according to a predetermined outcome. He expresses confidence in God's power, faith that the future outcome will be a good one. Thus, no matter what, because he fully accepts whatever outcome is in store, he cannot be made to feel angry, dejected, disappointed, bitter, or upset. This isn't to say that all outcomes are equal to him. Nowhere in this epistle does it sound as if he's weary of life and wants to die. And the poignant passages in which he expresses his longing to see his converts in Philippi again are a clear message that he wants to live long enough to see them again. But he is fully *accepting* of whatever outcome awaits him. The Spirit doesn't give you road maps or money-back guarantees of outcomes. What it promises is that "all things work together for good to them that love God" (Romans 8:28).

Let me share a story told by Elder Alexander B. Morrison that expresses what I mean:

> In late 1987, Robert E. Sackley, then president of the Nigeria Lagos Mission, felt that the time had come to move the Church north and west from its center of strength in the eastern states of Imo and Cross River. One of the cities he decided to open was Enugu, the former British capital of eastern Nigeria. He felt certain that among the inhabitants of that lovely place were the elect of God, waiting to be taught the gospel.
>
> About forty miles north of Enugu is the city of Nsukka, where the home campus of the University of

Nigeria is located. President Sackley had heard that a professor at the university had been affiliated with the Church in America. He even had the man's name: Dr. Ike Ikeme, a Nigerian.

Elder Sackley and his wife made a 140-mile journey to see Dr. Ikeme. He was not at the university when they arrived, but one of his coworkers took the Sackleys to his house to see him.

The Sackleys drove up to Dr. Ikeme's house and knocked at the door. It was opened by a man who glanced first at the car with the Church logo on the side and then at President Sackley. When President Sackley said, "I'm looking for Dr. Ikeme," the man replied with a smile, "I am Dr. Ikeme and you are the mission president. Welcome. I have been waiting six years for you." He then introduced his wife and three small children to President and Sister Sackley. Delighted to have found his man, President Sackley said, "Dr. Ikeme, are you a member of the Church?"

Dr. Ikeme said that he was, that he had been endowed six years earlier and had been attempting to live a Saint-like life ever since. His wife, Patience, was an educated woman with a master's degree in nutrition. She had been determined not to marry anyone for a while, certainly not someone from Kenya, but Ike was persistent and on their first date, in response to a question, he told her he was a Mormon. She asked him what a Mormon was. "You just watch me," was his reply.

On hearing this story, the Sackleys asked Patience, "Well, after six years of marriage and three children, what have you learned by watching your husband?" Her reply: "I have learned the Church is true. It is true because my man is true. Nothing that he would be involved with could ever be untrue, and no other religion on earth could cause him to live the wonderful life he lives in our home." . . .

Ike Ikeme . . . told President Sackley, "I want Patience to be taught the gospel without any pressure from me. I want her to accept the gospel for herself and not because of any influence I might exert." . . .

On November 19, 1987, Patience Ikeme was baptized by . . . Ike, and confirmed a member of the Church by President Sackley. Just six months later Ike Ikeme was called to preside over the Enugu District of the Nigeria Aba Mission.[5]

Now, think of the situation Dr. Ikeme was in. Alone in a foreign country, he joined a strange Christian church, participating even to the point of being endowed and taking upon himself sacred obligations, which had the potential of seriously affecting his relationship with his future wife. Think of the strength of his testimony as he left the support system of the Church's wards, temples, patriarchs, and publications and returned to his country where, as far as he knew, he might live the rest of his life as the only member of the Church. With no support, no communication, no one watching him, either to encourage him in well-doing or to chastise him if he went astray, he married and conducted himself so like a disciple of Christ that his wife, without knowing more than the name of the Church, knew that she wanted to become a member too.

This is a beautiful example of accepting the future with faith, feeling confident that, in the grace of God, our future will be a happy and a blessed one.

I don't know what you face in your future. For most it is

marriage and parenthood and grandparenthood. But for some, it will be singleness and childlessness. For some who are married, even in the temple, that marriage may end in divorce or abandonment. Even very happy marriages, like mine, can be interrupted by death. Perhaps some of you who are now in economic peril will find a secure future. For others, changing circumstances may bring economic insecurity. Educational challenges, job changes, unemployment, promotions, illness, accidents, meeting professional challenges, and probably failing at a few are predictably some of the surprises, both pleasant and unpleasant, that the future holds.

Can you remember Paul and fully accept whatever your future holds?—not because all options are equally preferable but because, if you face them with faith, the ending of the story will be a happy one.

It is well known that President Howard W. Hunter learned quite a bit about adversity through the long, gradual illness of his first wife and his own health challenges. Just before he became president of the Church, he gave a beautiful talk in general conference in which he addressed the topic of adversity:

"Jesus gives [this] invitation to all of us. 'Take my yoke upon you,' he pleads. In biblical times the yoke was a device of great assistance to those who tilled the field. It allowed the strength of a second animal to be linked and coupled with the effort of a single animal, sharing and reducing the heavy labor of the plow or wagon. A burden that was overwhelming or perhaps impossible for one to bear could be equitably and comfortably borne by two bound together with a common yoke. [Christ's] yoke requires a great and earnest effort, but for those who truly are converted, the yoke is easy and the burden becomes light.

"Why face life's burdens alone, Christ asks, or why face them with temporal support that will quickly falter? To the heavy laden it is Christ's yoke, it is the power and peace of standing side by side with a God that will provide the support, balance, and the strength to meet our challenges and endure our tasks here in the hardpan field of mortality."[6]

How can any of us face the future without the companionship and comfort of the Holy Spirit? For all of us, even the very young, death will come. We do not get to choose how we will die. For some, it will be unexpectedly, by accident, without warning. For others, disease will gradually fill our lives with such pain and weakness that death will come as a blessed release. For some, age will have robbed us of physical functioning and even our memories long before our bodies forget how to live and we step across the threshold into eternal life. As believers in Christ, we can accept even the likelihood of a grim future because we know that physical suffering and even death are only temporary—that through Christ each of us will be resurrected. Then, if we have been obedient to the commandments and endured to the end, we "shall have eternal life, which gift is the greatest of all the gifts of God" (D&C 14:7), that is to say, we will live forever in a glorified, resurrected body in the presence of our beloved Heavenly Parents and our Savior. What a glorious prospect!

Finding Contentment in the Present

The third point I want to make comes from Paul's epistle to the Philippians. He says: "I have learned, in whatsoever state I am, therewith to be content. I know both how to be abased, and I know how to abound: every where and in all things I am instructed both to be full and to be hungry, both to abound and to suffer need. I can do all things through Christ which strengtheneth me" (Philippians 4:11–13).

This truly is a great concept. It means that we can be patient with our circumstances and patient with ourselves and even patient with the Lord. Although Paul lacked physical freedom, he was contented because he could still preach the gospel. As someone once remarked, "I've learned that the Lord didn't do it all in one day. What makes me think I can?" Now, you may think that this was the wisdom of great age speaking, but the person who shared this piece of information was only forty-six.[7] So contentment is a great gift that we can seek at any age.

Does this mean that we should be content with our sins? Or content with our current level of education? Shouldn't we set goals and try to improve ourselves and our circumstances? That's not what Paul is saying at all. Remember that he expressed acceptance of his future, no matter what it was, because he knew that he had very little control over the outcome. He also had very little control over his present circumstances. Other people had usurped his right to decide where he lived, what he ate, when he ate it, whom he could speak to, whom he could write to, whether he could have paper and ink for writing—all kinds of things. Paul had virtually no control over his external circumstances, and he chose to be content within those limitations.

But on those matters where he *did* have control, he made significant choices. When he got to write a letter to the Philippians, he made it a letter of powerful faith and testimony. He expressed the profoundness of his love for the Savior and also his love for his converts. Sixteen times—or once every six and a half verses—he spoke of joy, gladness, and rejoicing. Now that's a significant choice.

All of us have limitations. None of us is completely wise, completely good, completely safe, completely righteous. We make mistakes all the time. And all of these are reasons why we should fine-tune our ability to listen to the Spirit. Circumstances may give us limited choices and options. When we have the ability to change some of our circumstances, then those are choices we should cherish and exercise. But even within severe limitations, we still have choices.

Think for example of the limitations imposed by chronic illness. I recently met a lovely and cheerful LDS woman who had chosen to make the most of her circumstances. She has multiple sclerosis, a progressive, degenerative disease. She has four children, and for twenty years she has been completely bedfast, unable to walk or even to sit up. She taught her children how to keep house and cook from her bed.

Yet she can talk, laugh, sing, and move her hands. So within these limitations she has found ways to find contentment and keep pushing against those limitations. For instance, she has a calling. She teaches Relief Society lessons on the fifth Sundays. She tapes her lesson on an audiocassette and will say, for instance, after she has discussed an idea: "Please stop the tape and turn to such-and-such a reference. Please read it out loud, then discuss what this idea means." Or she'll assign quotations to be read. The Relief Society president told me that on the fifth Sunday, women come who don't attend any other lessons.

She has a job. Because she can talk on the phone, she takes all the calls for the repairmen at an appliance store and transmits them to the dispatcher.

Because she can move her fingers, she crochets. Every new baby in that ward gets a fluffy, handmade shawl from her. People flock to see her, but she insists on being just as independent as it's possible to be. Her children are grown and her husband works, but her husband prepares her food and leaves it at her bedside with water that has a long drinking tube so that she can feed herself during the day.

She's an amazingly cheerful person. We spent so much time laughing when I visited her. I really enjoyed her and it was almost impossible to remember that this was a person who hadn't been able to walk for twenty years.

This woman is a gallant and heroic person because she has chosen to be.

We often hear about people who have suffered from chronic physical conditions who have not just endured their afflictions but are positive, happy, loving individuals. We hear less often about the suffering caused by mental illness. That's a situation in which many people have even fewer choices. An estimated 52 million Americans suffer from a mental disorder at some point during any given year. That's one in every five families.[8] Is there any reason to believe that LDS families are somehow immune from these emotional and neurological problems? I don't think so.

I'm far from being an expert on mental illness. I do know that although some forms can be controlled with proper medication and therapy, others must simply be endured. And when a loved one is mentally ill, everyone suffers. One psychologist, writing about schizophrenia, with which 43,000 people are diagnosed each year, writes: "The numbers fail to evoke the human suffering and personal tragedy which goes on, year after year, for those who recover only partially or not at all.

Schizophrenia is a sentence as well as a diagnosis. The result is often a life sentence for both the person afflicted and for the family. No release. No parole. No time off for good behavior."[9]

One woman whose mother was mentally ill spent her childhood feeling confused, hurt, socially isolated, and deeply ashamed of her mother's illness. Her mother was delusional, talked and giggled to herself almost constantly, felt obsessed that Australia was going to be conquered, and thought that she had to save it. She kept trying to fly to Australia. Most painfully, she believed that her daughter was a dangerous stranger who was trying to kill her.[10]

There were not many choices that this mother could make—often not even whether to take her medication or not. But the daughter had daily choices about how she would treat her mother, and whether she had enough love and patience and forbearance to care for a woman who didn't even know her. That was a choice she made in her present circumstances about how to deal with the difficult limitations that had been imposed on her. She could have made different choices: to institutionalize her mother permanently, to move to a far dis-tant town and cut off all contact with her mother, to remain ashamed and embarrassed by her mother's mental illness. I think that, with the aid of the Spirit, she chose a course that might be much harder in the short run but which will bring her greater happiness in the long run. I think individuals like this, who are providing care for the mentally ill, deserve our admiration and support.

Or think about aging. This is a topic I can relate to since I'll turn seventy-six in 2002. It's a condition that poses so many challenges that probably most of us wouldn't choose it except that the alternative to getting older probably isn't all that much fun either. Sister Camilla Kimball, who had a wonderful sense of humor, once joked, "Old age is not a status to enjoy, because there's not much future in it." Then she added, "Now that my memory has faded a bit, I can enjoy reading a book the second time. I enjoyed rereading the biography of my husband and, as I read along, I kept wondering how it would all turn out!"[11]

But for many, aging is a process that gradually erodes the personality and strips away dignity. These are harsh limitations indeed, forced on us by the circumstances of mortality.

Or think about the times we suffer as the result of other people's choices. A few years ago I attended the funeral of one of the Church's grand old men, Brother Sato. He and my husband had been good friends, and they visited together often. Brother Sato was the first man to be baptized in Japan after World War II, and he also made the first Japanese translation of the Book of Mormon. He reminisced often about the inspirational experiences he had had translating the Book of Mormon. I thought he might feel sad when a new translation was authorized; but after it came out, he read it and announced, "It's okay" and then got this big smile on his face.

After Ed's death, when I would visit him, Brother Sato would always say, "Take care of yourself. Exercise your face. That way, you stay young." He would rub his face vigorously with both hands, saying, "I do this every day." (My personal feelings are that when you live as long as Brother Sato and me, having a young-looking face is just going to confuse people, but I loved getting this advice from Brother Sato as my "beauty consultant.")

Brother Sato was the same age as President Benson and died in June 1996, four months before his ninety-seventh birthday. He had endured much suffering in his life, but he always hungered to know the truth; and long before the gospel came to Japan, he had become a scholar and a believer. As a youth, he met an American Methodist minister who was courageously telling the Japanese people about Christ, even though it was very dangerous to proselytize in Japan at that time. Brother Sato was baptized at age eighteen. He studied English in college, even though his major program was chemistry, and visited or attended many Christian churches, even though he joined none of them. That was where he first began translating religious documents from English to Japanese. He married his beloved wife, Chiyo, in 1924. He was involved in metallurgical research when World War II broke out. They had a son and a daughter, but the daughter died of malnutrition and dysentery following the war. If there had only been a little medicine available, her life could have been saved.

But as the American army of occupation moved in, Brother Sato encountered his first Mormon, a soldier who jumped off a Jeep, stuck out his hand, introduced himself, and announced, "I am a Mormon." Brother Sato didn't know very much about Mormons; but in November 1945, he met three American soldiers who walked four miles from their base in the town of Okazaki to Narumi, where Brother Sato lived. He took them into a tea house so they could get warm and offered them some coffee. They replied, "We don't drink coffee." Next he suggested, "Well, would you like to smoke some very poor Japanese tobacco?" Once again, they declined, saying they did not smoke. Lastly he said, "I know. I have some very fine Japanese tea." Once again, the soldiers declined. Then Brother Sato said, "You must be Mormons." They said they were and asked how he knew. Ironically, it was because the Narumi town drunk, years before, had told him about meeting a Mormon elder named Heber J. Grant who did not drink coffee, tea, or alcohol.

These faithful soldiers taught Brother Sato the gospel. When he learned about the premortal existence and postmortal life, he wept, telling the soldiers, "Now I know that we will have our little girl again." On 7 July 1946, Brother and Sister Sato made baptismal robes out of white silk that had been part of their little daughter's clothing and were baptized, the first baptisms in Japan after World War II. A twenty-year-old soldier named Boyd K. Packer baptized Sister Sato. That was the beginning of more than fifty years of service in the Church and for the Church for the Satos.[12]

Conclusion

Think of a choice as simple as that of a favorite crayon. It reminds us that our ability to hear the Spirit depends completely on our choosing to do so. Think of the Apostle Paul in prison, choosing to rejoice despite the adversity of his circumstances.

Then remember that we have choices, too. We often do not have choices about our circumstances. They are forced upon us and we must deal with them whether we want them or not. But if we will listen to the Spirit, we will understand that we do have choices to make about what we do within those limitations—just as Paul had choices within the walls of his prison. His choice was to accept the future with faith that God could turn it to blessing, whether that future involved freedom to preach the gospel wherever he went, freedom to write to his former converts from the prison, or death.

And third, we have choices about how to live within our limitations. Please remember that there are limitations of the mind and spirit more crippling than those of the body.

Remember the woman whose mother was mentally ill.
Remember Brother Sato, watching his daughter die of a simple
illness because there was no medicine or food. These are hard
realities to face.

Choose to face the future with faith because the Spirit will
be with you. Choose contentment in your present by listening
to the Spirit. Choose to love and support each other so that
there will be respite from the limitations that we suffer. May
we "look forward . . . having one faith and one baptism, having
[our] hearts knit together in unity and in love one towards
another" (Mosiah 18:21). And may we "exercise faith in the
redemption of him who created" us and look forward to hearing his voice say, "Come unto me ye blessed, for behold, your
works have been the works of righteousness upon the face of
the earth" (Alma 5:15–16).

NOTES

1. Associated Press, "Crayon Trivia," in "Trends" column compiled
   by Cherrill Crosby, *Salt Lake Tribune*, 2 February 1997, E-1.
2. Janet G. Lee, winter devotional, 14 January 1992, 1. Photocopy
   of typescript in the author's possession.
3. Ibid., 1–2.
4. Ronald Kelly and Paul Kroll, "Joy, Hope, and Love: Paul's
   Message from Prison," *The Plain Truth*, February 1994, 5.
5. Alexander B. Morrison, *The Dawning of a Brighter Day: The
   Church in Black Africa* (Salt Lake City: Deseret Book Co., 1990),
   93–96.
6. Ibid.
7. H. Jackson Brown Jr., comp., *Live and Learn and Pass It On*,
   vol. 2 (Nashville: Rutledge Hill Press, 1955), 114.
8. Sybil Shalo, representative of the National Alliance for the
   Mentally Ill, quoted in Kareena Johnson Wilding, "It's Crazy
   Maggie," *The Plain Truth*, February 1994, 9–10.
9. E. Fuller Torrey, as quoted in ibid., 10.
10. Ibid.

11. Camilla Eyring Kimball, "Women of Faith," in *A Heritage of Faith: Talks Selected from the BYU Women's Conferences*, edited by Mary E. Stovall and Carol Cornwall Madsen (Salt Lake City: Deseret Book Co., 1988), 3.

12. George M. McCune, "A Tribute to Brother Tatsui Sato." Pamphlet in the author's possession.

6

GENEROSITY IN GIVING
AND RECEIVING

$\mathcal{O}$ne of the greatest blessings the gospel offers us is the opportunity to both give and receive from the depths of a thankful heart. But this is a topic on which there's also a certain amount of sentimental nonsense. I like this story:

Thanksgiving Day was approaching, and the family had received a Thanksgiving card with a painting of a Pilgrim family on its way to church.

Grandma showed the card to her small grandchildren, observing: "The Pilgrim children like to go to church with their mothers and fathers."

"Oh, yeah?" her young grandson replied, "so why is their dad carrying that rifle?"[1]

Let's first consider giving, then discuss receiving—and let's talk about realities, not about sentimentalities.

Giving

Some of you may feel that you have little to give; and compared to the generosity of philanthropists who have organized entire foundations to help them make wise use of their charitable giving, I'm sure that's true. But all of us are rich in some ways. May I suggest some ways in which you are rich?

First, you are rich in appreciation. One writer tells this story:

"The other day I was in a hotel dining room where an orchestra was playing. It was a good orchestra, offering well-chosen selections, well played. On the way out, impulse prompted me to stop and say, 'Gentlemen, I have thoroughly enjoyed your playing.' For a second they looked almost startled. Then all of their faces broke into smiles, and I left them beaming over their instruments. My own day went off better for it, too.

"Another discovery I have made is that it is almost impossible to give away anything in the world without getting something back—provided you are not *trying* to get something. Usually the return comes in some utterly unexpected form, and it is likely to be months or years later.

"For example, one Sunday morning the local post office delivered an important special-delivery letter to my home, though it was addressed to me at my office, and the post office had discharged its obligation by attempting to deliver it there. I wrote the postmaster a note of appreciation. More than a year later I needed a post-office box for a new business I was starting. I was told at the window that there were no boxes left, that my name would have to go on a long waiting list. As I was about to leave, the postmaster appeared in the doorway. He had overheard the conversation [and asked], 'Wasn't it you who wrote us that letter a year or so ago about delivering a special-delivery to your home?'

"I said it was.

"'Well,' [he answered], 'you certainly are going to have a box in this post office if we have to make one for you. You don't know what a letter like that means to us. We usually get nothing but kicks.'

"I had a box within the hour. Bread upon the waters!"[2]

Think of all the opportunities you have to express appreciation. You have parents. You may have a spouse. Perhaps you have children. You have colleagues. You have teachers. You have friends and fellow ward and stake members who share their strength and their values with you. You interact every day with people who serve the public—such as clerks and bag boys and social workers; some of them, at least, provide genuine service. The letters to the editor columns are full of complaints and protests—and I'm not saying that some of them aren't justified. But every few days there's a letter of heartfelt thanks from someone who has no direct way to say "thank you" for a rescue, for the kindness of a Good Samaritan, or for an anonymous act of common decency.

So you have encouragement to give for the price of a postage stamp or, if it's in person, for absolutely free. You can be lavish in your gratitude. You can be prodigal in your appreciation. You can afford to!

The second quality with which you can be generous and prodigal is time. You have just as much time as the richest person on earth. You have just as much time as the most righteous person on earth. You have as much time as your mother or the governor of the state or President Hinckley or the chief justice of the Supreme Court.

And the gift of time is one of the most precious gifts you can give because it's the least renewable of resources. One woman gave her husband a magnolia tree for his birthday. He came home from the office early and found the part-time handyman there unexpectedly—it wasn't his regular day to work—digging a hole in the front yard. The workman explained, "I've never been able to give much, but I want to give you something. I'm going to give you this hole." The man said, "I never appreciated a present more."[3]

Those of you who are parents can relate to this story about a busy minister who was trying to write a sermon when one of his sons kept coming into his study. The minister offered him several items to distract him—a pencil, a quarter. But the boy kept coming back. Finally, the father asked, "Son, what *do* you want?" The boy replied, "Daddy, I just want you."[4]

And here's a third story. One writer said that one of his friends is a rich woman who has literally "everything that her heart fancies. One day I heard her mention some trifle that would require a tiresome downtown journey that she had no time to make. I felt that here at last was something I could do for her. I was astonished and touched to see tears of pleasure in her eyes as she said, 'To think of your going all that way for *me!*'"[5]

"Generosity doesn't require money. It requires imagination. It takes the ability to put yourself into the head of someone else, to recognize your spouse's weariness, your friend's anxieties, your grandson's fears, your mother's silent dreams, the anxiety beneath the cheerful smile of the woman you visit. When you can feel their feelings, then you can also feel what would ease their burdens. And when you have that kind of generosity, you will be much loved and therefore truly successful.

"[There is] the generosity that rejoices in another's good fortune. And the generosity of tolerance, which enables one to see things from another's viewpoint. . . . There is the generosity of tact, which avoids the thoughtless word or deed; and of patience, which listens to another's tale of woe; and of sympathy, which shares the burden of disappointment and grief.

"Perhaps the greatest of all generosities is that which gives the benefit of the doubt—which refuses to retail malicious gossip, which believes the best rather than the worst."[6]

If you have a thankful heart, then you have a heart that is constantly delighted with the mercies and blessings of God. When God is pouring out his riches upon us without stint and without stopping, then how can we feel other than rich in return? We are wealthy, philanthropic, beneficent, liberal, bountiful, and munificent. I love these words. Even their sound is generous.

Let me tell you a personal story. Soon after being released from the Relief Society general presidency, I received an invitation to speak in California, where I had the wonderful opportunity of spending some time with the sisters of the San Diego California Stake. My hostess, Sister Neeley, said, "Do you really have to leave Sunday?" It turned out that her daughter-in-law had arranged for a speaker from Salt Lake City to come and address a women's fireside in *her* ward, but the speaker had had an emergency and wasn't able to come. Would I go and give the same talk that I had just given to the sisters in San Diego?

Well, a lot of thoughts flashed through my mind as she asked this question. In San Diego, they had asked me to speak on the theme of "A Disciple's Heart." I had had almost two months to prepare, and I had worked hard and prayerfully on a talk that dealt with the challenges of avoiding hypocrisy and of following Jesus' teachings. As part of that presentation, I took with me some leis made out of seashells, which had been made by the sisters in the Islands and given to me with much aloha when I visited there. I passed these leis on, as a connection between those wonderful Hawaiian sisters and sisters sitting in the congregation whom I had never seen before and whose lives I did not know.

There was a special spirit in that chapel. They received this gift of love from their unknown sisters with added love from me. Afterward the stake Relief Society president told me that one of the leis had gone to a sister who was a recent convert, who had not fit in very well in her ward and had quite a sharp tongue. The president said she thought there was perhaps no one who needed an extra gift of love as much. And two of the leis went to women who were deaf and who had often felt excluded and left out. I felt really strongly that I was guided to them.

But of course, I didn't have any more leis. Furthermore, I usually like to think about and pray about a group of sisters that I'm speaking to and shape a talk to their needs, so when Sister Neeley asked if I would speak at Del Mar and use the same talk, I hesitated. I lifted my heart in a quick, silent prayer asking if this service would help those in the congregation and whether the concept would work in a different setting, without leis. The answer I got was a fragment—just a fragment— of a quotation from a scripture. It said: "If ye have desires to serve . . ." Well, I did have a desire, even though I had no preparation time and no leis. I said yes.

And that's when the miracle happened. After I finished speaking in Sister Neeley's stake, there were workshop sessions for the rest of the morning that were just delightful. One of the sisters who had been able to come to the opening session but then had had to leave was Nicole Richardson. She had gone home and made five little angels about two and a half inches high with a pearl head and wires curving down to make their robes. She sent them back with her sister, who came up to me at lunchtime and said, "Nicole said I had to come and give these to you. She loved the idea so much of the sisters making leis with love and giving them to you and you passing them on. She wanted to give something back to you with love. You don't know what your message did for her."

Well, I knew what her angels did for *me*, and I told her sister so. At Del Mar, I shared that story and then gave Nicole's angels to five sisters in the audience. Again, they were strangers to me, chosen completely at random. Afterward the Relief Society president told me that one of them was a sister in desperate need. She was so depressed that she had tried to commit suicide several times. Her husband would take her to her mother's when he went to work every day so that she would not be alone. She was a beautiful woman who had sung in the choir and had a gift of song, but had been struggling with her feelings for a long time.

I don't imagine that her problems were solved by a little angel, but I know it helped her to know that another sister whose name she didn't even know had felt enough love to reach out to her through me and that God knew where she was sitting in the chapel and wanted her to have one of those angels.

Afterward her mother also sought me out and thanked me. It wasn't me. It was God. I was willing to serve, even though I didn't know how I could. I said yes, not out of confidence but out of that willingness. And the Lord was able to make a miracle out of it. If you want to have a thankful heart, put yourself in the position of letting God answer someone else's prayers through you.

Now, think of what you have to share. Many of you with elderly parents or friends are keenly aware of what a blessing it is to have your eyesight, to have a car, and to be able to drive in traffic as you take your mother or someone else to doctors' appointments or to do some shopping or on an outing. These are activities that they can no longer do for themselves, and these are activities that we will some day require assistance to help us perform as well.

Sometimes, when I'm giving a talk, I'll ask a friend to participate with me by taking a cup to the closest faucet or drinking fountain, filling it, then bringing it back. I always have the cup right there and I always tell her it's not an emergency—she doesn't have to hurry, and the cup doesn't have to be filled to the brim, just to the level where she can walk with it comfortably. But I tell her that we're all going to wait while she's doing it, and that I'm going to time how long it takes.

Well, it seldom takes more than three or four minutes, but you can imagine how slowly those minutes pass while everyone is waiting. Then I explain.

I'm a member of the board of trustees of the Ouelessebougou-Utah Alliance. Ouelessebougou is the southern part of the country of Mali, in West Africa, close to the Sahara Desert. There are only three seasons there: the rainy season, the dry season, and the cold season. Cold means that the temperatures rise to the mid-80s by day and drop to about 55 degrees at night.

It's all comparative, isn't it! There are definitely times when we would think of those temperatures as very pleasant. I had a wonderful experience once of visiting Alaska where the temperature had been 40 degrees below zero earlier in the week. The sisters were so concerned that it would be too cold for me, that they had been praying very sincerely for the temperatures to ameliorate; and they considered that their prayers were answered when the temperature rose to 20 degrees above zero. "It's a heat wave!" they said.

But in Ouelessebougou, fifty-five degrees above zero is as low as it gets. Before the cold season, from June to September, comes the rainy season when it is very hot and rains every day. The third season is the dry season, from February to June. "Winds blow terrible dust storms across the plains. It is very hot, 95 to 130 degrees."[7] In Ouelessebougou, "women sometimes have to walk six miles to find water that is so dirty that people feel full after drinking it. One woman was bitten by a snake as she went for water, and she died."[8]

They have to carry this water home in jerry cans or plastic jugs on their heads. The average person can walk about three miles in an hour. You all know how much a gallon of milk weighs. How much water could you carry on your head for six miles? Especially if you were also carrying a baby on your back? And especially if, in addition to the baby, you were also pregnant? Think about it the next time you turn on the faucet or bend over a drinking fountain.

The Ouelessebougou-Utah Alliance has intervened at this very basic level to provide village wells. "Most traditional wells have gone dry, and whole villages have been forced to relocate because they have no access to water. . . . Men were often killed while digging [new wells] when the walls would collapse on top of them." During the rainy season when the ground becomes saturated with water, wells would frequently collapse, too. The Alliance wells are a real partnership. The villages show that they are serious about bettering their condition by digging the wells by hand to a "safe depth. Alliance drilling equipment is then brought in to reach clean water at depths of up to 100 feet. Concrete rings with a cover are inserted into the well for safer, more stable construction that will not collapse."[9]

Because there is enough water, the villagers can grow their basic food crop, millet. Because the women are spared the task of hauling water, they have enough time to cultivate vegetable gardens, which makes for a better balanced diet with more vitamins. Because the men have more time, they can build fences around the gardens to keep the goats out. Because the children are healthier, they can go to school. One small step leads to another.

Here is the day of an average village woman of Ouelessebougou: "Get up at first light, about 5:30 A.M. Go to village well, hand pull buckets of water. [This is obviously a woman fortunate enough to live in a village with a functioning well.] Pour water in container for bathing. Make fire from wood and brush. Heat rest of water in pan over fire. Add ground millet. Cook one hour. Hear baby waking. Clean baby, fasten in sling on back. Feed extended family. Clean up after breakfast. Pound lunch millet one hour. Stop to care for baby. Cook millet two hours. Walk to garden, baby on back. Hand pull buckets of water. Hand water garden. Pick okra and lettuce. Take lunch to men working in field. Walk to bush to cut firewood. Carry home large bundle of wood balanced on head. Pound millet for dinner two hours. Go to well, hand pull buckets of water. Build fire. Cook millet two hours. Make sauce, feed family dinner. Clean up after dinner. Pound millet for breakfast one hour. Go to three-hour literacy class. 11 P.M. Walk home in darkness. Sleep."[10]

I share that, not to make you feel guilty over how much

abundance we enjoy, but to stir up a feeling of gratitude. I'm not much interested in guilt, and I'm definitely not interested in making anyone feel guilty. I'm interested in helping us feel grateful.

A grateful heart is a happy heart, and a grateful heart is a generous heart. When we're grateful, we find it easy to share what we have because we *recognize* what we have. Without question, every person reading this page is literate. Most of us don't think of the ability to read as a prized skill, a rare possession. But for the women of Ouelessebougou, literacy is so precious that they are willing to give up sleep after a physically exhausting day to gain it.

Once we start thinking from an attitude of gratitude with a heart quick to appreciate, we realize that we have an enormous number of things to share.

What would my cup of water mean to a thirsty woman who had to walk six miles for it? When Jesus was trying to explain the concept of service to his apostles, he said, "And whosoever shall give to drink unto one of these little ones a cup of cold water only in the name of a disciple, verily I say unto you, he shall in no wise lose his reward" (Matthew 10:42). He was saying that the simplest thing makes a difference.

Receiving

I think that the gospel easily teaches most of us to be glad in giving and to rejoice in the brightness of possessing a generous and happy heart. But sometimes it is hard for us to receive. Do you ever get flustered or embarrassed when someone pays you a compliment or thanks you for something? Sometimes we don't know what to say. Sometimes we feel embarrassed because we're being singled out for attention. Sometimes we feel uncomfortable and awkward because we don't know how to respond, and that makes our response awkward.

Now, it's true that some gifts are exploitive. Some people give gifts to place the receiver under an obligation. Some people substitute gifts for honest communication. Instead of saying "I'm sorry" or "Can we be friends?" they hope the gift will speak for them. Whenever we sense a double message behind the gift, we naturally feel uneasy and uncomfortable. But I'm not talking about those situations. I'm talking about times when our own awkwardness hampers us from responding graciously to genuine generosity.

I choose to feel that any real gift, any service, any compliment is really sending the secret messages: "I love you. I admire you. I respect you." I think those secret messages are the messages we should respond to. It's a message about the relationship, not about the object.

When we respond with embarrassment or awkwardness or over-effusively to a gift or a service, we are sending back the message: "I don't want you to notice me. I don't need or want your love. I don't want a relationship. I don't want to be connected to you."

Could I suggest that instead we respond to the message behind the gift or service or compliment?

Let me share with you two stories from the scriptures about a gracious response. The first is from the Old Testament, the story of David. Bethlehem is called the "city of David" because it was his birthplace. This incident happened during the Philistine wars, when the Philistines held Bethlehem, and David was camped outside the city.

"And David longed, and said, Oh that one would give me

drink of the water of the well of Beth-lehem, which is by the gate!

"And . . . three mighty men brake through the host of the Philistines, and drew water out of the well of Beth-lehem, that was by the gate, and took it, and brought it to David: nevertheless he would not drink thereof, but poured it out unto the Lord.

"And he said, Be it far from me, O LORD, that I should do this: is not this the blood of the men that went in jeopardy of their lives? therefore he would not drink it" (2 Samuel 23:15–17).

The scripture does not record that David thanked the men for bringing him the water at the peril of their lives, but could they have had any doubt about his appreciation of their gift? He did not just say, "Gee, guys. This is really swell water." He said, "This water is sacred, so sacred that it is worthy to be offered to the Lord in sacrifice. It is holy to me." And isn't the rest of the message clear and obvious? "And the relationship that you have established with me this day is holy to me, too."

In the second story, Jesus received a precious gift:

"Then Jesus six days before the passover came to Bethany, where Lazarus was which had been dead, whom he raised from the dead.

"There they made him a supper; and Martha served: but Lazarus was one of them that sat at the table with him.

"Then took Mary a pound of ointment of spikenard, very costly, and anointed the feet of Jesus, and wiped his feet with her hair: and the house was filled with the odour of the ointment.

"Then saith one of his disciples, Judas Iscariot, Simon's son, which should betray him,

"Why was not this ointment sold for three hundred pence, and given to the poor?

"This he said, not that he cared for the poor; but because he was a thief, and had the bag, and bare what was put therein.

"Then said Jesus, Let her alone: against the day of my burying hath she kept this.

"For the poor always ye have with you; but me ye have not always" (John 12:1–8).

Again, there is no record that Jesus said, "Thank you, Mary. This was really very thoughtful of you." He probably did express his thanks in some way, but we know the value that he put on the gift because of what he said in rebuking Judas Iscariot. He said, in essence, "Mary has given me a gift that will ease even the pains of the death I must die. It is a gift whose sweetness will overcome even the odor of the death that awaits me." And remember, when Lazarus was in the sepulchre and Jesus had come to raise him, he talked separately to each sister—both to Mary and to Martha, asking if they had faith. And each one of them did. It was to Martha that Jesus said, "I am the resurrection, and the life" and it was Mary who said to him, "Lord, if thou hadst been here, my brother had not died" (John 11:25, 32).

They knew that he was the master of life and death. Lazarus was sitting at the table next to Jesus, restored to the loving care of his sisters by the Lord's hand. If anyone in that room needed proof that the Savior had power over death, Lazarus was a breathing, eating, talking visual aid.

Yet Jesus graciously accepted this costly gift, this lavish expensive present. He let Mary wipe his feet with her hair. He announced that she was doing it for his burial, and Matthew adds the sentence, "Verily I say unto you, Wheresoever this gospel shall be preached in the whole world, there shall also this, that this woman hath done, be told for a memorial of her" (Matthew 26:13).

What was Jesus really saying to Mary? He was saying: "You know *me*. You understand me. You know who I am." Here, in a house crowded with people, occurred a moment of such intense intimacy that I think we cannot even understand it. We all long to be understood and accepted for who we are. Jesus, who was not mortal in the same way we are, still must have longed for that mortal feeling more than most mortals— precisely because he was *not* mortal. How many times did people look on him and see who he really was? Those moments, as recorded in the scripture, are rare moments of personal revelation to someone whose spiritual eyes were opened to see beyond the homeless man, the homespun robe, and the dusty feet in their simple sandals. Mary had given him a gift much more precious than the precious ointment, and he was letting her know that she had.

Think about the significance of these two stories. In each case, the thanks of David and the thanks of Jesus reached beyond the gift to the relationship. In the examples cited earlier in this chapter, we considered the kind of generosity that takes not one penny but instead takes your most precious non-renewable resource—time, which when coupled with tact, sympathy, and loyalty, becomes the gift of a relationship. They say: "I am with you. I am for you. I'm on your side." And do you know why these are the most precious gifts to give or to receive in a relationship? It's because these are the gifts that come from the "personhood" of the giver and that affirm the "personhood" of the receiver. These are types of the endlessly charitable, abundantly generous, unstintingly lavish gifts the Savior gives to us.

God's spirit of love is with us. He loves you—oh, how he loves you—for the righteous desires of your heart, for the good that you do, for your hunger to serve him and bless his children.

But more than that he loves *you*. He loves *who* you are. He loves you unconditionally. He loves the whole you, *all* of you, not just the good parts or the disciplined parts or the parts that serve. He loves your history, even if your past has been sorrowful and painful, not just the present of service and the future of righteousness that we all long for. He is with you. He wants you to feel him with you, to trust him enough to acknowledge his presence, not just in your moments of strength or joy or private meditation but also in your hours of pain and moments of selfishness and times of despair and self-loathing. Yield your heart to him. Let him heal you. Let him fill you with joy and consolation.

We hear a lot about being willing to sacrifice so that we can serve. Yes, it *is* true that service takes willingness to sacrifice some selfishness. But I know that whatever we have to share is acceptable to God, and I think the most marvelous illustration of this principle is a story told by Richard Stanford, a fifty-year-old businessman in Atlanta, who related an experience he had when he was taking the public rail system to work. Normally his schedule meant that he missed the rush hour, but that particular morning, he'd had to take a different train. While he was waiting to change trains at the connecting point for the east and west trains, he realized that he was standing in a crowd of perhaps a thousand commuters, all waiting for their trains, and literally the only sound he could hear was "the hum of the escalators." No one was talking. Then he heard a woman's voice:

"'Good morning!'

"The greeting echoed through the station. A thousand heads snapped up in unison. . . . The voice had come from a woman riding the descending escalator on the far side of the platform.

"'How y'all this morning?' She practically sang her words. . . . People began to turn toward her.

"The petite African-American woman reached the bottom of the escalator and walked purposefully to the edge of the throng. She grabbed a surprised businessman's hand, shook it, and looked him in the eyes. 'Good morning! How y'all doing this morning?'

"The man looked at the small woman who had him in her grip. He broke into a smile. 'Fine, thank you.'

" . . . She moved through the crowd, shouting greetings, shaking hands, and laughing freely. Finally, she looked across at the crowd on my side of the platform. 'How y'all folks over there this morning?'

"'Just fine!' I shouted back. Others answered with me. We surprised each other so much that we broke out laughing.

"'That's good,' she said. She paused and looked around. Now everyone was listening. 'God sent me here to cheer you up this morning. And that's the God of the Jews, the Christian, the Muslim, and any other religions y'all brought or didn't bring along.'

"From where I stood, I could see a twinkle in her eye. Amazingly, the train station came alive to good-natured conversation. As we chatted with each other, few noticed the slight woman quietly ascend the up escalator."

Stanford went on to describe the effect this woman's unabashed friendliness had on him and others. People who normally wouldn't have spoken to each other or even acknowledged each other's presence found themselves interacting, chatting, smiling at one another.

He summarized the experience by saying, "I felt happy and alive."[11]

Well, there was a little sacrifice involved in that service, wasn't there? The petite African-American woman had to sacrifice her fear that she might be laughed at as crazy. Richard Stanford had to sacrifice his shyness and his isolation. All of those people who ended up chatting and laughing with each other had to sacrifice a few minutes of reading their newspapers or remaining in their private thoughts. But how much of a sacrifice was it really? And what did they get in return for the sacrifice? When we are willing to give and receive, then we receive something we can always pass on and multiply in the lives of others.

Now, I suggest that we have an absolutely unlimited number of smiles to share. And I've never heard of anybody who has run out of "Good morning's" or hugs either. So may I suggest that each of us become a one-volunteer dealership for all three in our homes and neighborhoods and see what happens? If one small woman coming down an escalator can make a thousand strangers smile and talk to each other, what might we do?

Conclusion

An anonymous writer has observed:

Many people seem to believe God has called them to live successful lives. In fact, He calls each one of us to live *faithful* lives—lives of obedience, devotion, worship, and service.

With each day there often remains a residue of things left undone, unsaid, unachieved, or unconquered. Each day has its own measure of failure, its own degree of trouble (see Matthew 6:34), and its own lingering doubts.[12]

The important point is that we don't need to impose the burden on our lives of judging ourselves against some standard of perfection. God asks us only to live each day with gladness as the day he has given us. Whether it's a successful day or not does not lie completely in our power. Successful compared to what? If we receive each day from God's hands and give it back to him at the end of the day in that same trusting way, there's no end to the good God can do with it in between.

Think about giving with a generous and sympathetic heart. You will not wonder if your gift is needed or appropriate because your sympathy will tell you the needs of each person and your generosity will enable you to give a unique gift of yourself—a sacred gift, a holy gift, a gift that affirms the relationship.

And you will not feel awkward or uneasy about receiving, because you will understand that the true gift behind the gift is a gift of love. And you will know how to respond to that gift, because the voice of God will whisper how to you.

NOTES

1. Quoted in *Holy Humor*, edited by Cal and Rose Samara, (Carmel, California: Guideposts, 1996), 183.

2. David Dunn, "Try Giving Yourself Away," originally printed in *Reader's Digest*, August 1945, undated reprint in the author's possession, 134–35.

3. I. A. R. Wylie, "The Secret of True Generosity," undated article, reprinted from *Reader's Digest*, June 1954.

4. Ibid., 77.

5. Ibid., 76–77.

6. Ibid., 78.

7. Ouelessebougou-Utah Alliance Calendar, illustrative page for April 1998.

8. Ibid., August 1998.

9. Ibid.

10. Ibid., May 1998.

11. Richard Stanford, "Escalator Angel," in *Chicken Soup for the Christian Soul: 101 Stories to Open the Heart and Rekindle the Spirit*, compiled by Jack Canfield, Mark Victor Hansen, Patty Aubery, and Nancy Mitchell (Deerfield Beach, Florida: Health Communications, Inc., 1997), 297–99.

12. Anonymous, "Faithfulness," in *Sunset with God* (Tulsa, Oklahoma: Honor Books, 1996), 178–79.

7

"BE STILL AND KNOW
THAT I AM GOD"

Psalm 46:10 reads: "Be still, and know that I am God: I will be exalted among the heathen, I will be exalted in the earth." Verse 11 continues: "The LORD of hosts is with us; the God of Jacob is our refuge." In other words, this verse answers an unconscious question: "How will being still help us know God?" And that question in turn leads back to still another question: "We must be making noise. Why are we doing that?"

Well, obviously, we're making noise because we feel alone and afraid. We feel that we don't have a refuge. We are crying or weeping or whimpering softly or shrieking with terror or pain. But regardless of the manner in which we're being *unstill*, it's preventing us from knowing God. The Doctrine and Covenants expands our understanding of this principle by repeating the injunction to "be still and know that I am God" but then adding some important explanations:

"And they that have been scattered shall be gathered.

"And all they who have mourned shall be comforted.

"And all they who have given their lives for my name shall be crowned.

"Therefore, let your hearts be comforted concerning Zion;

for all flesh is in mine hands; be still and know that I am God"
(D&C 101:13–16).

Do you think the scattered ones felt lonely? I do. Do you
think that the mourning ones felt that their world was full of
words of grief and tears of sorrow? I do. So it is in the context
of real problems and real feelings about those problems that
the Lord repeats: "Let your hearts be comforted concerning
Zion; for all flesh is in mine hands; be still and know that I am
God."

This scripture offers great comfort. It points us away from
the problems and fears and anxieties that perplex us and that
fill our minds with turmoil and our mouths with chatter and
lamentation. It lets us concentrate, if only for a moment, on
the face of Christ himself, leaning over us in love and encouragement and promise. In that moment of stillness, miracles
can happen; in response to the Savior's love, peace and knowledge and strength can flood our souls.

To take the image one step further, consider something
the Lord told the Saints of Joseph Smith's day: "Wherefore,
lift up thy heart and rejoice, and cleave unto the covenants
which thou hast made" (D&C 25:13). Brothers and sisters,
when we know that Jesus is God and that all flesh, including
us and our children and all the other people we're so worried
about, are in his hands, how can we avoid lifting up our hearts
and rejoicing?

It is a great privilege to make promises to the Lord, as we
do in our baptismal covenant and in the weekly renewal of
that covenant through the sacrament. The covenants we make
in the temple, the covenants of marriage, and the sealing
covenants are additional promises between us and our loving
Heavenly Father. And all of them give us reason to rejoice.

In the moment of stillness in which we recognize the Savior, our testimony is born; but it grows only as we nurture it. As I have explored this idea in the scriptures, I have been impressed that this "lifting up" not only expresses our faith but also strengthens our faith. I want to share three ideas related to this concept—lifting up our hands in service, lifting up our heads in courage and good cheer, and lifting up our eyes in faith to the Savior. All of these things can bring us to the precious moments of stillness in which we see and recognize the face of the Savior—in which we know truly that he is God.

Lifting Up Our Hands to Serve

In Paul's epistle to the Hebrews we read these injunctions for brotherly and sisterly service: "Wherefore lift up the hands which hang down, and the feeble knees; and make straight paths for your feet, lest that which is lame be turned out of the way; but let it rather be healed. Follow peace with all . . . and holiness, without which no [one] shall see the Lord" (Hebrews 12:12–14).

What does it mean to "lift up the hands which hang down"? To me, this scripture conveys an image of terrible fatigue and weariness, of someone who simply does not have the strength to pick up a tool or a burden one more time. More than that, when your hands are hanging down and when your knees are feeble, you are easy to knock off balance. It is easy for you to lose your footing, to slip and fall. This is an image of someone who is simply at the end of his or her resources— beaten, broken, discouraged, downcast, and on the point of collapsing.

As I visit wards and stakes in some areas of the United States, I am impressed that some of us enjoy a disproportionate share of blessings. For the most part, we are well fed,

well clothed, well housed, and well educated. I remember visiting areas of the missions in Polynesia and Latin America
where many of the sisters would look at our quiet, orderly,
peaceable lives and think that we are already in heaven.

One of the wards I have lived in is an affluent ward, filled
with beautiful homes and wealthy people. But heartache can
cross those thresholds easily, too. One of the sisters whom I
used to visit teach was a lovely woman, but she had not come
to church for many months. I'll call her Gail. After her children were grown and out of the home, she slipped into a
depression from which it seemed very hard for her to extricate
herself. She had one daughter in the same town; but she and
this child had had a stormy relationship, and they were not
close. Her husband, a businessman, traveled almost constantly,
so she was home alone a great deal. There were many women
in the ward who were willing to be her friend, but they were
reserved about offering their friendship first and there didn't
seem to be a good way to make an overture. I knew none of
this when I was assigned to be her visiting teacher. Sometimes
a Relief Society president is inspired to give a visiting teacher
the whole background, and sometimes she's inspired not to.
I think this was one of those second cases.

When I was asked to visit Gail, I had a feeling to go immediately, without waiting for my companion. So I materialized
on Gail's doorstep and rang the bell. After a time, she came to
the door and opened it. I said, "Hello. I'm Chieko Okazaki.
Guess what? I'm your visiting teacher!" She was so surprised
she took a step back from the door. I promptly took a step forward, and that meant I was inside her home.

So she asked me to sit down; and the first thing you know,
we were having a good conversation. As we visited, she

became increasingly animated. At the end of the visit, I said, "I'd like to come back if you'd like me to."

And she replied, "Yes, I'd like that very much."

I began calling Gail every few days from the office. Her voice usually sounded dull and apathetic at the beginning of the conversation but more cheerful and lively by the end. I inquired about the medication she was taking and listened to her as she explained her sad and complicated feelings about her daughter. She refused to consider coming to church, read the scriptures, or pray, but I always prayed for her, night and morning, in my personal prayers. When my husband, Ed, died, she sent a sorrowful card of deep sympathy. I was able to talk to her husband, who was worried about her but not sure what to do, and also to her daughter, who began making cautious phone calls to her mother.

Then one night about 10:30, I suddenly had a feeling that Gail was in trouble. I was ready for bed, but I telephoned her. The phone rang for a long time before she answered, and she sounded confused and muddled. I thought at first she had been asleep, but I could hear a television playing in the background. "Gail," I said, "Gail, are you all right?"

"Yes," she said. "I'm all right."

I realized I had asked the wrong question. Gail was a woman who had lived her whole life denying the reality of certain parts of it and not acknowledging what they meant. So I asked again, "Gail, do you want me to come over?"

"Yes," she answered. "Yes, I'd like you to come over."

I threw on my clothes and was there in five minutes. It took her a long time to come to the door. Her clothes were untidy and her hair wasn't brushed. She looked disoriented and terribly downcast. She couldn't remember the last time she had eaten anything, and I suspected that she had simply forgotten to eat. Her husband had left her and was then living in another state. I made her show me what pills she had taken. She said she had only taken the prescribed amount, but I knew she had taken more because she kept drifting off to some other world in the middle of the conversation.

I heated some food for her and coaxed her to eat it until she realized she was hungry. I sat with her until one o'clock in the morning, and she grew more alert as we talked. Finally I felt that it was safe to leave her. She promised to go to bed and sleep. She also promised to go see her doctor the next day. When I called the next morning to check on her, she had already made the appointment.

I don't know if Gail was actually in danger, but I think she might have been if she had continued to sit in front of the television screen, with her pills close at hand, absentmindedly taking one, then another one. Fortunately, she began seeing a therapist after that and allowed herself to be hospitalized. I wish I knew the ending to the story, but when her husband came back, suddenly, within one weekend, they were gone. No one knew her address. I sent her a card and a couple of notes, which I assume the post office forwarded, but she never answered.

I tell you this story for two reasons, and one of them is not to suggest what a great visiting teacher I was.

No, the first reason I tell you this story is that I think we all want to do the right thing in our callings and make a difference in people's lives. I believe it was because I always prayed for Gail that my heart was tender enough toward her that I heard the voice of the Spirit whispering that she needed help.

The second reason I share this story is that it's not a tidy story with a happy ending. It's a story without any kind of ending. We all like stories with a happy ending. We'd like to know that she and her husband developed a warm and loving relationship, that she and her daughter were able to forgive each other and be reconciled in a strong mother-daughter relationship, and that Gail is now teaching Relief Society in the Mesa Arizona Second Ward or wherever she lives. Well, we don't know any of these things.

It's wonderful when real life is like an inspirational story, but often it's not. Gail had many problems when she came into my life. She had many problems when she went out of my life. I didn't solve any of those problems for her, but—and this is the important point—I was with her while she endured those problems. I was with her while she coped with those problems— even though she didn't cope very successfully with them. I was with her on those rare occasions when she turned away from denial and admitted that she had problems and took a few very tentative steps toward solving them.

I did what I could while I was with her. I did not despise her for having problems. I didn't scold her for not solving her problems. I didn't give her good advice about what she should do and then get huffy when she didn't take it. I was with Gail—listening to *her*, praying for *her*, extending my love to *her*.

Each one of you knows someone in trouble. Each one of you knows someone who needs help but who isn't being helped. I want to tell you with all the energy of my soul that your knowledge means that you have a responsibility to that person. That person may be in denial, but you cannot compound her denial by your own and still retain the Spirit of the

Holy Ghost. You can drown out the stillness in which God speaks by filling up the moment with chatter such as "Yes, but . . ." or "I don't want to" or "I'm afraid," but something within you is telling you to hush those voices and know God and what he wants you to do.

If you have been hesitating about doing *anything*, because you can't do *everything* to fix the situation, now is the time to act. You're not called to fix things or save him or her. You're called to listen, to pray for this person, and to be with him or her. Sometimes that's all we can do. Most of the time, if you've noticed, that's what the Savior does for us, so that, choice by choice, decision by decision, effort by effort, line upon line, we learn what to do with our free agency here in this wonderful world. And having someone with us while we do it makes it easier. Do you remember that beautiful scripture in Ecclesiastes about the strength to be found in working together?

"Two are better than one; because they have a good reward for their labour. For if they fall, the one will lift up [her] fellow: but woe to [her] that is alone when [she] falleth; for [she] hath not another to help [her] up. Again, if two lie together, then they have heat: but how can one be warm alone? And if one prevail against [her], two shall withstand [her]; and a threefold cord is not quickly broken" (Ecclesiastes 4:9–12).

You may be dealing with someone with feeble knees and hands that hang down. Perhaps this brother or sister has brought the problem upon him- or herself; but don't walk away and leave that person in his or her feebleness. Perhaps he or she is contributing mightily to the problem because of repeated bad choices or disobedience to gospel principles that are very clear to you. Don't despise, reject, cast out, or turn your back on this person. Be with him in his struggles. Give her your love. Pray with him and pray for him.

Lift up the hands that hang down, even if they are drooping again the next time you see them. Strengthen the feeble knees, even if he or she has strength for only one step. This is the Savior's way—undiscouraged and loving. When we follow his way, then we can truly lift up our hearts and rejoice because he will fill us with his love.

Lifting Up in Courage

The second way we can lift up our hearts and rejoice is to take stock of our own situation and have faith that the Savior is nearby to encourage us and strengthen us. The scriptures contain several important commandments about being lifted up to courage. For example, when the Israelites were preparing to cross over Jordan into Canaan, the Lord instructed Moses to climb to the top of Mount Pisgah "and lift up thine eyes westward, and northward, and southward, and eastward, and behold [the promised land] with thine eyes: for thou shalt . . . charge Joshua, and encourage him, and strengthen him: for he shall go over before this people, and he shall cause them to inherit the land which thou shalt see" (Deuteronomy 3:27–28).

In Job, we read: "Yea, the Almighty shall be thy defence, and thou shalt have plenty of silver. For then shalt thou have thy delight in the Almighty, and shalt lift up thy face unto God" (Job 22:25–26).

Consider this story about the courage that can come when we lift up our hearts unto God. Reed J. Webster, who was second counselor in the Johannesburg South Africa Temple presidency, received a call late one night from the first counselor. He had just received a message from the police posted in the train station that a Church member from Zimbabwe, who had been traveling for thirty-five hours, had just arrived, and no one could understand anything he said except "Johannesburg Temple." He had "a well-worn temple schedule and had asked the police officer to contact us."

President Webster took another missionary to accompany him. This was several years ago, and you know how terrible the violence and reprisals were in South Africa during that period of civil unrest. President Webster wrote: "We had to pass through areas that had been the scene of violence the night before and which were off limits to missionaries. The police were in full view that night with flashing lights and dog patrols. We parked our car . . . [and] chained up the steering wheel—a regular procedure."

The stern policeman at the train station thawed into warm smiles when they told him they were there for the man from Zimbabwe, and he began asking questions about the temple. This policeman had been so impressed by the calmness and serenity of the little man that he wanted to know more. The man was only about five feet tall. His name was Sandalamu Mikikafu Chisembe, he spoke a dialect they couldn't understand, and the letter he carried with him indicated that "he couldn't 'hear' English," as the letter said. President Webster continued, "But our spirits spoke to each other as though we were long-time friends." He had had someone write a letter in English for him, explaining that he was a branch president in Zimbabwe. The letter said, in broken English: "I have come to the temple to seek for spiritual power, for preaching, teaching, and doing all the Lord's work. . . . There are seven townships meeting at Mufakose branch for sacrament meetings. . . .

When missionaries teach the new members. It is our duties to do home teaching.

"We the branch president, first counselor, and all priesthood find it very difficult to go to members who are far away. Our buses are very unreliable. That is why I have come here to seek for solution. . . . I know that there's no other place to get spiritual power other than the temple.

"I had only a few dollars but through asking from the heavenly Father I have managed to come here. . . . So many big businessmen around the buildings where I work, but Heavenly Father chose me."[1]

President Webster was honored to take Sandalamu Mikikafu Chisembe to his home, to feed him and care for him, and to escort him to the temple the next day where he patiently sought for the answers he needed about the needs of the Saints in Zimbabwe. President Chisembe had lifted up his heart and had performed an amazing and miraculous feat of courage that armed men would have hesitated to undertake.

One of the scriptures that I always associate with the temple and with the covenants we make there is the glorious Psalm 24, which has been made into an anthem of victory:

"Lift up your heads, O ye gates; and be ye lift[ed] up, ye everlasting doors; and the King of glory shall come in.

"Who is this King of glory? The LORD strong and mighty, the LORD mighty in battle.

"Lift up your heads, O ye gates; even lift them up, ye everlasting doors; and the King of glory shall come in.

"Who is this King of glory? The LORD of hosts, he is the King of glory" (Psalm 24:7–10).

You may remember a few years ago when a man came into the BYU multi-stake fireside that was being broadcast by

satellite to Church Education System classes and interrupted
President Howard W. Hunter as he began his address to the
students. Claiming that he had the detonator to a bomb, this
troubled individual held President Hunter hostage for about
half an hour. The students in the Marriott Center began to
sing, "We Thank Thee, O God, for a Prophet," which seemed
to confuse this individual, and other students were able to distract him until the security personnel could take him in
charge. He turned out not to have any explosives, as you know.

President Hunter rested for a few minutes, then calmly
continued his talk. This talk was published in the October
1993 *Ensign* without any mention of the dramatic events that
had accompanied its first delivery. But in that context and
given President Hunter's remarkable coolness while he was in
a situation that might easily have been tragic for him and for
those present in the Marriott Center, I think the opening para-
graphs of his talk have deep significance. He said: "Despair,
doom and discouragement are not acceptable views of life for a
Latter-day Saint. However high on the charts they are on the hit
parade of contemporary news, we must not walk on our lower lip
every time a few difficult moments happen to confront us.

"I am just a couple of years older than most of you, and in
those few extra months I have seen a bit more of life than you
have. I want you to know that there have been some difficulties in my mortal life, and there always will be. But knowing
what we know, and living as we are supposed to live, there
really is no place, no excuse for pessimism and despair.

"In my lifetime I have seen two world wars, plus Korea,
plus Vietnam and all that you are currently witnessing. I have
worked my way through the Depression."

President Hunter then alluded to other problems and

continued by strongly encouraging his audience to accept the gospel as an anchor to their souls, to keep them steadfast in the midst of trials.[2]

I do not pretend that we live in untroubled times. There are troubles all around us. But I am saying that if we can be still, we will know that God exists. We can lift up our hearts to the Savior and can rejoice. Remember that he is "mighty to save" and that if we will lift up our eyes to the hills, we shall see that our help comes from him (see 2 Nephi 31:19).

If our hearts are fixed on the Savior, we will have a solid reason to rejoice, to rejoice in spite of adversity and to rejoice even *in* our adversity. Sometimes we make our burdens heavier because we think we shouldn't have problems. We feel guilty. We compare ourselves to Sister So-and-So, who seems like a model of perfection, and our knees become more feeble and our hands droop a little further. Brothers and sisters, we don't need to compare ourselves to anyone else. We are okay, just the way we are, each of us, with our own needs, our own abilities, our own desires for righteousness, and our own set of obstacles to overcome. I want you to recite my favorite Japanese proverb from the ancient book of Okazaki, chapter one, verse one: "Lighten up!"

If you're doing the best you can, that's good enough. I don't know many men and women who aren't doing their absolute level best in every way, but plenty of them keep track only of the things they *don't* do perfectly. Many people I know accomplish a phenomenal amount, but often they don't pay attention to what they've done. Rather they concentrate on what's left undone or what remains still to do. Their hearts are literally downcast. They have given their hearts to their burdens, not to the great Helper and Lifter of burdens.

Now "lighten up" isn't a message that says, "Be irresponsible." It's a message for those who are already taking their responsibilities so seriously that they feel burdened and weighed down by them. Remember that lovely promise made by the Savior: "Come unto me, all ye that labour and are heavy laden, and I will give you rest. Take my yoke upon you, and learn of me; for I am meek and lowly in heart: and ye shall find rest unto your souls. For my yoke is easy, and my burden is light" (Matthew 11:28–30).

How can the burden be light? It's because the yoke is a double one, designed for two. Jesus wants to be our yokefellow, and instead we struggle on, insisting on pulling the whole load ourselves, never realizing why it feels so lopsided. The Savior wants to share that burden, and we need to let him.

I want you to memorize my ancient proverb and keep it handy when dark moments come. Let the sunshine into your lives. Don't be hard on yourself, and don't let other people be hard on you, either. Give yourselves credit for the good things you do. If you make a mistake, give yourself credit for trying. Laugh a lot. Catch yourself singing. Whistle or hum as you go about your duties. If you only do half of what you wanted to do, or only do it half as well as you'd like, pat yourself on half your back. But lighten up!

When you feel *dis*-couraged, when all of your courage has leaked away and you feel downcast and your lower lip is getting too close to your jogging shoes, I give you permission to pat yourself on the back for what you are doing. The Savior did not suffer in Gethsemane and die on the cross to rebuke you, to chastise you, to turn his back on you, and to despise you. He did all of these things so that he could redeem you and save you and lift you up to meet him in the clouds of glory at his second coming, "and so . . . ever be with the Lord" (1 Thessalonians 4:17). That is the glorious message of the gospel to all of us.

Lifting Our Eyes to the Savior

We've talked about lifting up our hands in service and lifting up our hearts in courage. But I think the most important lifting that we can do is the third kind of lifting: lifting up our eyes in faith to the Savior and then waiting in stillness to know that he is God.

There is a beautiful prayer in Psalms by someone who had faith in God and yearned for even more: "I stretch forth my hands unto thee: my soul thirsteth after thee, as a thirsty land. Hear me speedily, O LORD. . . . hide not thy face from me. . . . Cause me to hear thy lovingkindness in the morning; for in thee do I trust: cause me to know the way wherein I should walk; for *I lift up my soul unto thee*" (Psalm 143:6–8; emphasis added).

When we lift up our soul to God, is it possible that we can remain cast down in gloom and misery? No. Certainly our troubles will not vanish, but we will see them differently and we will have the strength to bear them better.

Do you remember the experience of Alma when he had been cast out of the city of Ammonihah? He was "weighed down with sorrow, wading through much tribulation and anguish of soul," when an angel appeared to him. What was the message of the angel? He said: "Blessed art thou, Alma; therefore, lift up thy head and rejoice, for thou hast great cause to rejoice; for thou hast been faithful in keeping the commandments of God" (Alma 8:14–15).

In other words, the Lord did not judge Alma because of his success or lack of it in the city of Ammonihah. The hard-heartedness of the people of Ammonihah was their own problem, not Alma's. The angel's message for Alma was one of praise and blessing for his years of faithfulness.

Several years later, when Mormon was bidding farewell to his own noble son, he counseled him: "My son, be faithful in Christ; and may not the things which I have written grieve thee, to weigh thee down unto death; but *may Christ lift thee up*" (Moroni 9:25; emphasis added).

In 1836 in Kirtland, during a time of great trouble in the newly restored Church in our dispensation, Joseph Smith related this beautiful vision as part of his record of the dedication of the temple:

"I saw the Twelve Apostles of the Lamb, who are now upon the earth, who hold the keys of this last ministry, in foreign lands, standing together in a circle, much fatigued, with their clothes tattered and feet swollen, with their eyes cast downward, and Jesus standing in their midst, and they did not behold Him. The Savior looked upon them and wept."[3]

Why didn't they see him? Because they did not lift their eyes. And the Savior also wept. I'm sure he wept in sorrow for their sufferings, but I think he also wept in sorrow because he could not comfort them. Do we have the faith to lift our eyes to the Savior, even in the midst of afflictions and troubles, and rejoice in his love?

One Christian writer explains the role of adversity this way:

"Suffering transforms, matures, and instructs. Suffering increases our capacities of love and understanding. All suffering makes us have something in common with any of those who suffer. It is a power of communion. Undoubtedly, suffering sometimes hardens us. It does not necessarily bring us closer to *virtue*. But it always brings us closer to *truth*. Suffering and death are the only two unavoidable obstacles which compel the most mediocre man to call himself into question, to detach himself from his existence, and to ask himself what would permit him to transcend it. What neither love, nor prayer, nor poetry, nor art could do for most people, only death and suffering are capable of demanding."[4]

Conclusion

Let me remind you in all soberness that we have accepted the covenant of baptism and that we also bear the name of Christ. We have agreed to walk in his way, to see with his compassionate eyes, to speak truth and love and comfort as if he spoke through our mouths, and to be his hands and feet in doing good to each other upon the earth.

We are called to serve others when we hear the Lord's words to lift up our hands. Think of my visiting teaching story—a story without a beginning and whose ending I may never learn in this life. If there is a Gail in your life—even if she's there for only two days or two weeks—walk beside her. Be with her in her dark places.

Second, the Savior calls us to lift up our heads in courage and good cheer. Remember that he is our yokefellow and that our burdens can be light when we let him infuse his courage in us and let him help us carry our burdens. We need not increase our burdens by adding inappropriate guilt to them.

And third, the Savior asks us to lift up our eyes in faith and behold his countenance. Remember the Savior, standing in the midst of the apostles who had given their all and suffered greatly to preach his gospel but whom he could not comfort because they did not lift their eyes to him.

One of the most beautiful blessings found in the Old

Testament is the gentle and loving benediction that the priests of Israel pronounce at the end of religious services:

"The Lord bless thee, and keep thee:

"The Lord make his face shine upon thee, and be gracious unto thee:

"The Lord lift up his countenance upon thee, and give thee peace" (Numbers 6:24–26).

I pray the same blessing upon us: that as we lift our countenance to the Savior's, that he in turn will lift up his countenance upon us, be gracious to us, give us peace, and keep us in his blessing and his love. In the stillness of that peace, may we truly know that he is God.

NOTES

1. Reed J. Webster, "Man of Few Words Radiates Serenity," *Church News*, 4 January 1992, 11.

2. Howard W. Hunter, "An Anchor to the Souls of Men," *Ensign*, October 1993, 70.

3. *History of the Church of Jesus Christ of Latter-day Saints, Period I, History of Joseph Smith, the Prophet by Himself* (Salt Lake City: Deseret News, 1904), 2:381.

4. Louis Evely, *Listen to Love: Reflections on the Seasons of the Year; Photographs, Poems and Readings,* compiled by Louis M. Savary with Thomas J. O'Connor, Ruth M. Cullen, and Diane M. Plummer (New York: Regina Press, 1971), 80.

8

FOLLOWING IN FAITH

or each of us to be faithful is one of the themes that President Gordon B. Hinckley has sounded during his presidency. He said: "The greatest thing we can do for the safety of our nation and to strengthen it is to cultivate within the membership of this Church stronger, ever stronger faith in the Lord Jesus Christ, that our people might walk in righteousness and become an example to all and be as the leaven to leaven the lump, as it were. Let us walk in faith and faithfulness."[1]

What kind of footprints does walking in faith leave? I'm sure the Church's sesquicentennial theme of "Faith in Every Footstep" made us wonder what kind of footsteps we were taking and what kind of footprints we were leaving behind us. Not dramatic, spectacular instances of faith like those we often associate with the pioneers of 1847, but everyday faith—my faith, your faith—faith in every footstep. The first thing that speaks powerfully to me is that little word *every*. "Every footstep" means that there's more than one footstep. It means that there's progress, effort, continuity.

A second idea is that we are not walking alone. Sometimes we're carrying a child, so that our effort is lifting two. And sometimes we've caught hold of a strong hand that is lifting us and pulling us along. But the point I want to make is that our line of footprints isn't the only mark on the path. The third question is perhaps the most important one. Where is our pathway going? What do we have faith in? Or more precisely, *whom* do we have faith in?

This discussion focuses on the faith we have in the Savior—the faith that strengthens us for the Tuesday mornings when it's raining on the newly painted fence, and the Friday afternoons when the battery has died in the car, and the Wednesday night when we choose to go grocery shopping at exactly the same time as every other consumer in the Western Hemisphere. I want to talk about *living* faith—not an abstract idea or noble ideal but a living, working, practical faith.

Let's consider three concepts: movement toward a goal, the relationship we should have with the people who are nearest us on this journey, and building our faith in the Savior.

Movement toward a Goal

First, let's discuss the direction our footsteps are taking us. We know our ultimate destination: we want to come unto Christ, to be the sheep of his pasture, the lambs of his fold. We want to enter heaven with a sense of welcome and homecoming that will tell us that we belong there and always have.

It's hard to keep our eyes on a goal. There are many distractions. There are many failures. There are times, I know, when it feels that we're taking one step forward and two steps backward, or that we're lurching to the right and the goal is slipping to the left. But I want to talk about the idea of progress.

Sometimes what we're really good at is being unable to distinguish the important stuff from the unimportant stuff and then beating ourselves up over the unimportant stuff. I was so

grateful for a mother who could tell the difference when I read
Wendy Udy's article in the *Ensign* about her fifteen-year-old
daughter, Adrienne, who had come home from stake conference feeling horrible about herself. The mission president, who
had been the last speaker, had praised the daughter of the
family in whose room he had slept the night before. He had
described the neatly arranged desk, the tidy shelves of books,
dolls, and stuffed animals, the handy note cards on which she
had written scriptures, and a card tied to her lamp on which
she had written "I am a daughter of God."

In contrast, Adrienne's room was undeniably a mess:
"Clothes spilled out of the closet and lay everywhere. Her
school books were scattered on the floor. Her desk was clut-
tered with containers of hair spray and perfume, candy wrap-
pers, old seminary homework, and an empty piggy bank. The
bulletin board above her desk was loaded with pictures of
friends and rock stars; it tilted at a rakish angle because of the
baseball cap hanging from one corner of it."

Her mother could only agree: Adrienne's room *was* a mess.
But Wendy didn't agree with Adrienne's conclusion. Con-
trasting her room with the excruciatingly tidy room occupied
by the mission president, Adrienne, in tears, wailed, "I'm no
good. . . . That girl the mission president was talking about [is]
a perfect person with a perfect room. . . . Nobody would ever
talk about me that way. I'm no good, and I know it. . . . I'm
sick of perfect people. I'm never going to go to church again."

Tenderly, this mother held her daughter and reminded her
that the piggy bank was empty because Adrienne had paid for
lunch for a friend who had no money. And one of the smiling
girls on the bulletin board had tried to commit suicide, calling
Adrienne after she had taken some pills. Adrienne made her

throw them up, insisting that she hold the phone by the sink so she could hear her. Then she made the girl call her sister, then called her back and stayed on the phone with her until the sister arrived.

Wendy reminded her daughter of that experience and what it revealed about her heart.

"Adrienne managed a smile. 'Maybe I'm not so bad then?'

"'You're not bad at all,' [Wendy] said, hugging her. 'Sometimes daughters of God can have messy rooms, and he loves them anyway.'"[2]

I love that message. Every woman in Relief Society and every girl in Young Women—young or old, healthy or ill, new convert or the descendant of many generations in the Church, is a daughter of God, a sister of Christ, the child of Heavenly Parents. And every boy and every man is likewise a son of God. And guess what? None of us is perfect. Each of us has to deal with the equivalent of a messy room somewhere in our lives. But that messy room is not the most important part of our lives.

I want to tell you an important fact. The Savior knows about your messy room. He's not shocked. He's not even surprised. He doesn't think you're a spiritual slug. He's waiting for the time when you're ready to open the door to that room and start stuffing things into a garbage sack. In fact, he'll hold the sack for you and make a few suggestions and laugh with you over some of the things you've been carefully preserving in that messy museum. He has confidence in you. He trusts you. He knows that you know what you need to repent of. He knows that you know the right thing to do. He's not going to blame you, accuse you, or scold you. He's going to help you.

What do you truly desire? What do you want to become?

If what you want is eternal life with the Savior, then miracles will happen in your life. Any weakness, any failings, any inadequacies, and any obstacles are only temporary so long as your heart is fixed on the Savior. Anatole France, the novelist and philosopher, said: "Some succeed because they are destined to; most succeed because they are determined to."[3]

Be determined to come unto Christ. No weakness of yours is as strong as his love for you. No failing on your part can put you beyond the reach of his mercy. No inadequacy is so great that his grace is not sufficient to make up the deficit.

So that is the first message I want to communicate. Make footprints. Make lots of footprints. Keep them pointed in the direction of the Savior, and don't worry if some of them wobble. If you move with faith in every footstep, you will look back some day and see that the course you have traveled is straight and true.

And especially, please don't think that you must make footprints exactly the same way that everyone else does. Every July, the Primary children sing that little song, "Pioneer children sang as they walked and walked and walked and walked. . . ." It may be one of the most truthful songs about the pioneer experience, but it also has to be one of the least fun songs to sing. Besides that, I *know* children. I'll bet there was a lot of skipping, jumping, hopping, running, and somersaulting going on, too.

I say this because some of you may feel as if you're permanently out of step. Some of you may be single in what seems like a married church. Some of you may be childless in a family-centered church. Some of you may be struggling in a ward where everybody else looks as if their toughest decision is which tie to wear to sacrament meeting. I'm here to tell you that you can do it your own way. It's okay to hop, skip, and jump. It's okay to stand on one leg and rest for a few minutes. It's okay to climb on a big rock and jump down like a mountain lion. There are many ways of being righteous. There are many ways of being Mormon. Being single is one of those ways. Being childless is one of those ways. Struggling is definitely one of those ways.

Only the Savior knows our hearts and only the Savior can judge us. In fact, he has specifically commanded the rest of us: "Judge not that ye be not judged." I am so grateful for this commandment. It relieves me of such an enormous and unwelcome burden of appraising, of evaluating, of labeling, of reproaching, and of criticizing. We don't have to approve of our neighbor's politics or lifestyle. We don't have to evaluate the parenting style or the homemaking skills or the career choice of anybody in our Sunday School class. We don't have to decide whether someone is following the prophet with sufficient rigor. We don't have to look around Relief Society when we enter it and label who is appropriately dressed or who should have taken her baby to the nursery or who is likely to make a comment in class that we won't agree with. We can just sit down next to the first sister that we come to, greet her with love and acceptance, help her if we see a need, and enjoy the spirit of sisterhood with her during the lesson.

And we also don't need to accept any judgments that people may make about us, either. We don't need to explain, defend, apologize, or justify. The Savior knows our hearts and that's good enough for him.

A sister from Oregon shared with me a talk she had given in Relief Society about the importance of understanding differences. She used her own life as an example, and it must have been one of the most vivid and engaging lessons that Relief Society had ever had. She and her husband were converts, drawn to the Church because they wanted their children to have a religious experience. They were impressed by the family orientation of Mormonism and were baptized just before Christmas in 1989. She writes:

"Little did we realize what exactly we had gotten into! It was a complete lifestyle change for us! I still feel like a baby—a newborn in the Church. I had such a tough time because I felt so different from everyone. I came from a very different background than *most,* not all, but *most* members. I came from a broken home in which no one believed in a God."

Ask yourselves how you would find charity and acceptance in your heart for this sister. Her mother was an alcoholic and a drug abuser. Her father was "horribly abusive." She left home on the day she was eighteen, but by then she had already experimented with drugs, alcohol, and promiscuity. Some of you may come from similar backgrounds. Do you feel that no one understands you? And those of you who grew up in happy, stable families—can you relate to someone from that background? Could you extend love and acceptance, even if you didn't understand everything? I think most of us would feel compassion and want to help her, but I think we might lack understanding.

We might think, *Well, that's a terrible background. How fortunate she is to have found the gospel. Of course she'll want to completely change herself and her personality right away.* We may not understand that she might not be able to change who she is right away. In fact, she might not *want* to change everything about herself immediately. Can we understand that she might just want to be accepted for who and what she is and then, in the safe space of that acceptance and love, begin to change herself?

Acceptance doesn't mean approving of her former lifestyle and personality. It means loving her *eternal* self and having faith that over time, and through living the gospel, she can and will change because her eternal self will desire righteousness and be drawn to it. She writes:

"When I joined the Church, I was completely overwhelmed. I felt completely different from everyone! I hated crafts and baking, I didn't particularly enjoy being a mother, and I wasn't perfect! You see, I perceived everyone in the church to be perfect and to have perfect lives. This was detrimental to me for I became discouraged and severely depressed. I felt stifled in such a homogeneous atmosphere! I thought that I must have been the only Democrat in the whole church; I certainly was the only one who swore up a blue streak when I stubbed my toe."

Feeling as she did, this precious sister did a perfectly natural thing. She stopped coming to church. What she didn't know is that she wasn't all that different. Periods of inactivity are actually not all that exceptional in the Church, even for people who have been members all of their lives—who are born to Mormon parents and baptized at age eight. According to a study done by the Research and Evaluation Department of the Church, "about seventy-five percent of lifelong Latter-day Saints experience a period of inactivity lasting a year or more." About sixty percent of them eventually come back.[4] These statistics suggest that we should have a lot of understanding and no harsh judgments for people who feel so uncomfortable at church that they don't feel they can come.

Most of them will eventually respond to our acceptance. And this sister was the same. She wrote:

"While away from the church, I had fun. I'm not going to lie to you. It was a sense of freedom to me, a release from all of the incredible guilt that I had been feeling. After months, seven to be exact, I decided that I had better go back to church because I was worried about the kids missing out. I went back haughty and rebellious. I had been unintentionally hurt by a few people, and I was very different, but I was going to show everyone that I was . . . proud of it!"

In other words, she had felt judged and it had hurt. But for her children's sake—not even for the sake of her own spirituality—she was ready to try again. She could see and feel something that she wanted for her children, and she hoped she could be accepted just for herself. She describes her own mellowing, how she tried not to judge others, not even those who hurt her feelings. She accepted them as having acted unintentionally and without personal malice toward her. But she also came to accept herself as she was—imperfect, struggling, but worthwhile and making progress. Her closing message is:

"I don't want you to think that this is a perfect and happy ending, because it's not. Every day is a struggle for me. A struggle not to swear, a struggle to pray, a struggle not to smoke my cigarettes, a struggle to deal righteously with my children, and a struggle to come to church on Sundays. But I'm taking it day by day: little bit by little bit; person by person; and situation by situation.

"I do love Jesus and his gospel, and I know he died for my sins, so there's always hope."[5]

Now, when we understand how hard she is trying, our hearts go out to her in love and support, don't they? My dear sisters and brothers, we never know enough to accurately judge anyone. Only God does. We just need to accept them, love them, share our faith with them, and serve them as best we can. One of the most important things we can share is the great joy and gladness that the gospel gives us. The gospel is good news, not bad news. And the Lord gave it to us because we are imperfect and we need it to help us be better, not because we are perfect and have no room to improve. The Savior loves each one of us, in our imperfections. He wants us all to be righteous, but each person has his or her own pathway toward being righteous. That's why we have been given the gift of the Holy Ghost, so that we can receive guidance on our individual paths.

Kindness

The second point I want to make is about the kind of relationship we need to develop with the people who are our companions on this journey. The first message was to encourage you, to invite you not to be hard on yourself or to cripple yourself by obsessing on your faults and failings as you attempt to move forward. It was a caution against becoming discouraged. Now I want to give you a complementary caution—one on the other side of the problem.

Please don't focus so intently on your celestial destination and be so determined to get there at any cost that you become heavy-handed and heavy-footed zealots, pushing other people aside or dragging them behind you as you hurry toward your goal. While you're making your footprints of faith, please don't step on other people's toes.

Think of Jesus. His whole life was directed toward the Atonement—toward that crushing but crowning night of betrayal, agony, and trial and that day of torment, thirst, and death. His life led straight to the cross, the tomb, and the upper room where he appeared, despite closed doors, to show his disciples his deathless body.

But the way to the cross was a gentle way. He did not press ruthlessly forward. Instead, he went from grace to grace, from service to service, from act of love to act of love. The way to the cross is made radiant and lovely by the blind man who saw men "like trees walking" after Jesus passed his way; by the weeping widow of Nain, whose tears of sorrow turned to tears of joy when her son was restored to her; by the five thousand fed on the loaves and fishes. Along that way there was a short and despised tax collector whom Jesus called down from a sycamore tree, a despised and much-married Samaritan woman to whom he gave living water, and a heart-broken father whose young daughter was restored to him.

Follow the Savior's example of kindness and love as you move forward with faith. The Relief Society motto is "Charity never faileth," and we're very happy to share it with the brethren as well. Truly has it been said that "charity is that with which no [one] is lost, and without which no [one] is saved," and "Charity is the pure gold which makes us rich in eternal wealth."[6]

Sometimes we erroneously think we have to be harsh on sinners to show that we reject sin. Fiorello La Guardia, once the mayor of New York City, is the hero of a story of mercy *and* justice that shows what I mean. On a particular evening, Mayor La Guardia had dismissed the night-court judge to hear the cases himself. It was one of the ways he stayed involved with the city, along with "riding fire trucks, accompanying the police on raids, and taking entire orphanages to ball games." It was a bitterly cold winter's night in 1935, just as the effects of the Great Depression were beginning to lessen. An elderly woman was accused of stealing a loaf of bread. The baker insisted, "She's got to be punished to teach people around here a lesson." The woman admitted taking the bread but explained that her grandchildren were starving. Her son-in-law had deserted the family, and her daughter was ill and could not work.

La Guardia announced: "I've got to punish you. The law makes no exceptions—$10 or 10 days in jail."

Then he reached into his pocket, pulled out a $10 bill and dropped it into his hat. He said: "Here's the $10 fine which I now remit: and furthermore, I'm going to fine everyone in this courtroom 50 cents for living in a town where a person has to steal bread so that her grandchildren can eat. Mr. Bailiff, collect the fines and give them to the defendant."

The bailiff turned over $47.50 to the old woman.

Policemen were present to testify in other cases. Petty criminals awaited trial. Citizens had come to appeal traffic violations. All paid the fine—and gave La Guardia a standing ovation.[7]

So, along with being kind to yourself, be kind to others. Treat them with the gentleness and love that Jesus showed. Provide the support and nurture that will make changing easier for them, not harder. Let the faith in your footsteps spill over to the faith of those around you as you move forward.

Having faith in the Savior

We've considered the direction we need to be moving—what constitutes progress—and we've thought about the people who are with us as we move forward on our journey. Now, let's talk about the third idea, having faith in our Savior.

March is an important anniversary to me. In March 1992,

I was pacing the halls of the LDS Hospital in Salt Lake City or sitting in a little windowless room with my two sons, waiting for those few precious minutes each hour when we were allowed into the intensive care unit where my dear husband, Ed, was lying unconscious. The day before had been the Relief Society's sesquicentennial celebration. Perhaps some of you saw the satellite broadcast of that program? Well, I'm afraid I can't remember much about it.

With our husbands joining us, the general Relief Society presidency had lunch together after the broadcast, delighted that the program in the Tabernacle had gone so well. Then, while we were strolling together back to our cars, Ed suffered a cardiac arrest. At one moment he was smiling, talking with Joe Jack. At the next, he was lying unconscious on the sidewalk.

Joe, who is a surgeon, immediately began CPR. We were only a few yards from the Church Office Building. The security guards came running and an ambulance was there within minutes; but Ed never regained consciousness, not then, not in the hospital. He slipped quietly away a few days later with no final farewell. I love the spring season and the Relief Society birthday, but it will always have bittersweet associations to me because of that experience.

I have always had a deep love for the Savior, ever since I joined the Church at age fifteen in Hawaii, and even before then when I was a skinny eleven-year-old Buddhist girl investigating the Church. But I had never clung to my faith so hard or prayed so earnestly as I did in the days while Ed was dying and then afterwards when I faced alone what seemed like a long, desert-like stretch of days, with each thirsty hour asking me how I was going to get through it.

I came to a new understanding of the sacrament prayer:

. . . that we may always have his Spirit to be with us. I claimed that promise. I leaned on that promise. And thank heaven for the work of the Relief Society that brought its own spirit of comfort and consolation.

On the day that Ed would have turned seventy-four, I took a bouquet of flowers to the cemetery. A foot of snow covered the ground. I could tell from a tombstone where his grave was and tried to dig through the snow to find the flower stand, but I had no success. Finally, I left the flowers lying on the grave and, cold and alone, went back to my house. On the way I sang the words to "Abide with Me! Fast Falls the Eventide." It is a hymn that has given me enormous comfort in the past several years, particularly the second verse, which says: "O thou who changest not, abide with me!" (*Hymns*, no. 166). And I felt that abiding.

Ed's death was a change I had to struggle with. I still struggle with it. We live in a time of great changes. All change, even when it is planned-for, worked-for, desired, and welcomed, can also be a struggle. Think of the birth of a new baby. Even when you're a very experienced mother, a new baby always brings many changes. Sometimes the changes are minor and temporary—like not being able to sleep through the night for several months. Sometimes, if the baby is sick or if the family has to move to a larger house, or if there's a particularly jealous sibling, the changes are longer lasting and can be much more demanding. But we need to be able to identify these inconveniences and problems as real and valid, even though the joy that the baby brings and the many tiny miracles that occur for everyone in the whole family outweigh the inconveniences and problems. Think about the changes that accompany graduation from college or getting a promotion where you work. Even when you've wanted that change and worked hard for it, there are necessary adjustments that come with it.

The point I want to make is that the Savior understands our joys and our sorrows. He abides with us. He abides without changing, during the times of our most trivial changes and the times of our soul-racking and painful changes. Our conditions and circumstances change very easily. Friends may turn against us. Loved ones may die. We may lose our health to disease or an accident. But one thing never changes—that is the love of the Savior. The Apostle Paul comforted the Hebrew Saints by saying: "[Jesus] hath said, I will never leave thee, nor forsake thee. So that we may boldly say, The Lord is my helper, and I will not fear what man shall do unto me. . . . Jesus Christ is the same yesterday, and to day, and for ever" (Hebrews 13:5–6, 8).

These words from the Old Testament remind us of the constancy of the Lord: "Set me as a seal upon thine heart, as a seal upon thine arm: . . . Many waters cannot quench love, neither can the floods drown it" (Song of Solomon 8:6–7).

The Savior is the seal upon our hearts so that we truly know that many waters of adversity—including the many waters of our own tears—cannot quench his love for us, as Isaiah reminds us: "Thus saith the Lord that created thee, . . . and he that formed thee, . . . Fear not: for I have redeemed thee, I have called thee by thy name; thou art mine.

"When thou passest through the waters, I will be with thee; and through the rivers, they shall not overflow thee: when thou walkest through the fire, thou shalt not be burned; neither shall the flame kindle upon thee.

"For I am the Lord thy God, the Holy One of Israel, thy Saviour: . . .

" . . . Thou wast precious in my sight, . . . and I have loved thee . . .

"Fear not: for I am with thee" (Isaiah 43:1–5).

Elder Bruce C. Hafen describes our being "spiritually sustained" by our relationship with the Savior each time we partake of the sacrament. "Through it, the Savior grants not only a continuing remission of our sins, but he will also help compensate for our inadequacies, heal the bruises caused by our unintentional errors, and strengthen us far beyond our natural capacity in times of acute need."[8]

Few of us will escape from this life without soul-searing and soul-searching crises. But sometimes I think it is easier to pull ourselves together and rise to the occasion because we know that our spiritual survival is in jeopardy and because other people are usually depending on us at these times of heightened crisis.

Sometimes it is far harder to deal with the normal, minor crises of everyday living. Not one of them is important in and of itself, but cumulatively these little pinpricks of disappointment can wound as deeply as the sharpest loss. Each task and expectation in itself is minuscule, but collectively they form a burden so heavy that they can buckle our knees.

Our challenge is not to be heroes and heroines in dealing with dramatic and traumatic circumstances as much as it is in being steadfast in the face of small but steady erosions of patience, with slight but increasing burdens, with abrasive worries, with fatigue, with loneliness, with being misunderstood and unappreciated, with discouragement.

I bear testimony that Jesus is with us in the daily-ness of our lives. He is with you when you've misplaced the car keys and are late for work. He is with you when your daughter needs help with her math and you've forgotten everything you ever knew about algebra. He is beside us as we deal with a budget that simply can't be stretched far enough, with patience that has already been stretched too far, with cheerfulness when the only alternative to laughter is tears.

None of these problems is overwhelming or discouraging or unmanageable by itself—only in combination and only when we feel that we are left alone without resources to cope. At times like these, please reach out to the Savior. He is not a marble statue standing aloof at the end of a stony path, waiting to see if you will make it. He is walking on the path beside you. If you listen, you can hear his voice, whispering encouragement to you, telling you that he has walked this path himself, calling his legions of angels to lift you up lest you dash your foot against a stone. We cannot be alone when he is with us.

Sometimes, as women, we think that there are parts of our lives that the Savior cannot enter, parts that he does not understand because we are women. This cannot be true, because his saving mission encompassed each and every soul that has ever been born on the earth or who will ever be born. He suffered in Gethsemane for the sorrows and sins and pains of each human being, and he knows the joys and sufferings of women, both spirit and body, just as much as he knows those of men.

He knows the anguish, both physical and mental, of the sexually abused child. He knows the sorrow of the childless woman. He understands the fear of abandonment, the wearing down that results from chronic illness and aging, the diminishment of being mocked and despised. Boys and men suffer through these experiences as well. They are *human* experiences, although we experience them from the built-in perspective of being male or female.

The message is for all of us: Jesus came because we needed a Savior, not because we were already perfect. Why do we think that he is more concerned about our neighbor than with us, or assume he has a special relationship with the Relief Society president because her calling is more important than ours? He has a special relationship with each one of us. Those who seem to be most in tune may just be those who listen longest. The Savior is never too busy to listen to us and respond. He has all the time in the world just for you. You don't need to stand in line or take a number or make an appointment or worry about having someone page him when you're halfway through. We're the ones who stand in line. We're the ones who are too busy. We're the ones who let ourselves be interrupted. We're the ones who think that hearing the voice of the Holy Ghost is a mysterious process and that we couldn't possibly learn how to do it as well as someone else.

Elder Jay E. Jensen shares some very important thoughts about how to listen to the Holy Ghost and know whether we're receiving an answer from the Spirit. He said:

"When the Holy Ghost speaks, our minds may be struck with insight and clarity akin to sudden light. At the same time, our hearts may turn or we may feel flooded with joy or deep gratitude or love. Whatever particular feelings occur, they occur simultaneously in the mind and in the heart.

"Some common expressions investigators often use during missionary lessons are 'That makes sense,' 'I've always believed that,' 'Of course.' Sometimes, it may be a simple affirmative nod. At these times, the investigators are experiencing 'enlightenment.' When we recognize the truth through the Spirit, we understand things—they become clear to us. As the Lord promised, 'I will impart unto you of my spirit, which shall enlighten your mind'" (D&C 11:13).

Elder Jensen also shares a story I love because it shows how homely and practical the voice of revelation can be:

"One Sunday, [a bishop] had had an unusually heavy day of interviews, meetings, and visits. It was near 10:30 P.M. when he had a chance to walk through the chapel past the pulpit. He felt so overwhelmed with the weight of his responsibilities that he dropped to his knees in the dimly lighted chapel and pled with God for strength to carry the load. While he was praying, a voice came to his mind: 'Bishop, you're so tired! Why don't you go home and go to bed?'"[9]

Now *that*, I submit to you, is a very significant revelation. Why do we assume that the Savior wants to be involved only in the gigantic decisions of our lives? Not so. Nothing is small that leads us to increased faith in him, and nothing is so large and overwhelming that you cannot face it better with the Savior at your side. We need faith to keep our perspective. Consider this poem:

> Within the eye, a nerve so small
> A feather would outweigh,
> Yet it brings into view the stars
> Ten billion miles away.
> Just so, within the heart, the eye
> Of faith brings into sight
> The unseen stars of glory
> In a world of truth and light.[10]

Conclusion

We've explored three concepts related to the concept of following in faith. First, don't get discouraged on the journey. Be gentle with yourselves. Remember Adrienne's messy room and keep the important things in perspective. Remember that you can do it your own way. Second, don't trample on others as you make your journey. Remember Fiorello La Guardia who found a way to uphold the law and live a greater law at the same time. And third, remember the whole purpose of moving forward in faith is to bring us closer to the Savior.

Let me conclude with the promises of the Lord to us if we will move forward with faith:

"[Let us look] unto Jesus the author and finisher of our faith; who for the joy that was set before him endured the cross, despising the shame, and is set down at the right hand of the throne of God.

"[Let us] consider him . . . lest [we] be wearied and faint in [our] minds.

"[And] let us lay aside every weight, and the sin which doth so easily beset us, and let us run with patience the race that is set before us" (Hebrews 12:2–3, 1).

"[For] they that wait upon the Lord shall renew their strength; they shall mount up with wings as eagles; they shall run, and not be weary; and they shall walk, and not faint" (Isaiah 40:31).

It is my testimony that the Savior is with us not only on the days of eagle wings but also on the days when we limp slowly, wondering if we will faint. And I promise you that his patience is longer and his love is greater than the race that lies before us and that he will renew our strength.

NOTES

1. President Gordon B. Hinckley, priesthood leadership meeting, Vacaville/Santa Rosa Regional Conference, *Church News*, 20 May 1995.

2. Wendy Udy, "Can a Daughter of God have a Messy Room?" *Ensign*, December 1996, 30–31.

3. Quoted in *To Your Success: Thoughts to Give Wings to Your Work and Your Dreams*, compiled by Dan Zadra (Woodinville, Washington: Compendium, Incorporated, 1994), 73.

4. Perry H. Cunningham, "Activity in the Church," *Encyclopedia of Mormonism*, 4 vols. (New York: Macmillan Publishing Company, 1992), 1:15.

5. Melissa Aniello, "Celebrating Differences," talk given at Tualatin Oregon Stake Conference, 2 May 1993, 2–4. Photocopy of typescript in the author's possession. Used by permission.

6. St. Robert Bellarmine and Jean Pierre Camus, *The New Book of Christian Quotations*, compiled by Tony Castle (New York: Crossroads, 1983), 32–33.

7. Greg Albrecht, "Making a Difference," *The Plain Truth*, February 1994, 14.

8. Bruce C. Hafen, "The Restored Doctrine of the Atonement," *Ensign*, December 1993, 12.

9. Jay E. Jensen, "Have I Received an Answer from the Spirit?" *Latter-day Digest* 2, no. 5, 5–8.

10. Helen Lowrie Marshall, "Organs of Vision," in *Walk the World Proudly* (New York: Doubleday & Company, 1969), 21.

9

SPARROW PRAYERS

I want to call your attention to little prayers. Perhaps it's more accurate to call them prayers for little things. I call them "sparrow prayers." The phrase comes from that wonderful expression of ultimate consolation and reassurance given by the Savior.

"And fear not them which kill the body, but are not able to kill the soul: but rather fear him which is able to destroy both soul and body in hell.

"Are not two sparrows sold for a farthing? and one of them shall not fall on the ground without your Father.

"But the very hairs of your head are all numbered.

"Fear ye not therefore, ye are of more value than many sparrows" (Matthew 10:28–31).

This scripture inspired a beautiful hymn of faith and reliance, written by Civilla D. Martin, who was born in 1860, the year before the Civil War broke out.

> Why should I feel discouraged?
> Why should the shadows come?
> Why should my heart be lonely
> And long for heaven and home
>
> When Jesus is my portion?
> My constant Friend is He;

His eye is on the sparrow,
And I know he watches me.

"Let not your heart be troubled,"
His tender word I heard,
And resting on His goodness,
I lose my doubts and fears;

Though by the path He leadeth,
But one step I may see,
His eye is on the sparrow,
And I know He watches me.

Whenever I am tempted,
Whenever clouds arise,
When song gives place to sighing,
When hope within me dies,

I draw the closer to Him,
From care He sets me free:
His eye is on the sparrow,
And I know He watches me.

The topic of sparrow prayers is a joyful thing to talk about, but the path to the joy leads through sorrow and even bitter sorrow, because we first have to deal with the question of seemingly unanswered prayers, and then the topic of building trust and faith when it may seem that there is little reason to believe and to trust. Come with me on that journey.

We know about the Lord's might and miracles. When the Lord made his covenant with Abraham and promised him that his posterity would be as the sands of the sea, Sarah overheard and laughed because she knew her body was too old to conceive a child. The Lord didn't stop to explain what he knew about ovulation and infertility. He simply said: "Is any thing too hard for the Lord? . . . Sarah shall have a son" (Genesis 18:14). And as we all know, Sarah *did* have a son.

Jeremiah praised God: "Ah Lord God! behold, thou hast made the heaven and the earth by thy great power and stretched out arm, and there is nothing too hard for thee" (Jeremiah 32:17).

Since we know that the Lord *can* do everything, and since we know that he has done mighty miracles in the past, how, then, do we explain the many times that our righteous prayers seem to go unanswered? Think of those heart-breaking, heart-stretching prayers. Think of your own missions or the missions of your sons and daughters who are teaching a promising family who has unquestionably felt the Spirit but who, for some inexplicable reason, turns away on the brink of baptism—or worse, accepts baptism but then falls away. Some of you are single. Many of you have prayed with sincerity and faithfulness, from the pure center of a righteous life, to find a worthy spouse, but your prayers have not been answered in the way you have hoped. Some of you have been carrying the burden of same-sex attraction; and despite your yearning prayers, the feelings do not go away. Some of you are struggling with chronic ill health, and ask yourself the terrible question of why you lack faith to be healed. For others, there are wounds of the soul and spirit left over from crimes inflicted on you in your childhood. These memories drain your strength and your will to continue.

Think of the burdens borne by others. Some women in the Church can relate to Sarah because they and their husbands are worthy, married in the temple, and have hearts open to welcome children to their home, but to whom children do not come despite their fervent pleadings. Think of the loving mother who yearns over her wayward daughter, but the daughter continues to make terrible choices that endanger her spiritual life and her physical life and even the life of an innocent child whom she may bring into the world. Think of parents who send their clean, strong son into the mission field, eager to serve the Lord, and who pray for his safety and success every day, only to have him fall prey to a casual criminal or to a drunken driver or to a disease that is not treated properly. Think of the sister who serves faithfully in the temple but whose last years are tortured by crippling illness and disease. Why do these prayers seem to go unanswered? In every ward, in every stake, you know people whose lives compel you to ask these questions.

Some people cruelly blame the person who is experiencing these difficulties, accusing her or him of not being righteous enough or not exercising enough faith. I refuse to blame the person who is suffering. It is a harsh and wicked judgment that lets the person who is saying such things avoid coming to grips with the fact that the prayers of the righteous are not always granted. I do not accept it. I know that sometimes the answer that the Lord gives us is "no" because he knows it will not be for our best good—but surely that is not the explanation in every case.

I *do*, however, think that there are three reasons that may help explain why prayers are not always answered in the way we might wish:

First, the scriptures do not tell us about all cases of infertility—only about Sarah's and then only because her story is important to the story of the patriarchs whose miraculous activities are recorded in scripture. In other words, Sarah's answered prayer may be the exception, not the norm. What about the hundreds of Sarah's sisters who endured childlessness for their entire lives?

Second, God cannot be compelled to answer our prayers the way we want him to every time. That would mean he is a machine and our only task would be to punch the right buttons. Or it would mean that he is like the genie in the lamp and our job is to say the right spell. No, he is free to act, and we are free to act.

Third, because we live in a world that operates according to law and because God's respect for agency is one of the most important facts we know about him, next only to his love for us, then there are some prayers of ours he cannot grant without violating the agency of others in ways that are unacceptable to the laws that govern our world. Because we cannot see all of the consequences of an action or a choice for ourselves, let alone for all of the people it might affect, there are doubtless some prayers he cannot grant.

But then what are we to make of all these ask-seek-and-knock promises?

"And all things, whatsoever ye shall ask in prayer, believing, ye shall receive" (Matthew 21:22).

"Verily, verily, I say unto you, Whatsoever ye shall ask the Father in my name, he will give it you. . . . Ask, and ye shall receive, that your joy may be full" (John 16:23–24).

"Ask, and it shall be given you; seek, and ye shall find; knock, and it shall be opened unto you:

"For every one that asketh receiveth; and he that seeketh findeth; and to him that knocketh it shall be opened" (Matthew 7:7–8).

"Therefore, if you will ask of me you shall receive; if you will knock it shall be opened unto you" (D&C 6:5).

"Draw near unto me and I will draw near unto you; seek me diligently and ye shall find me; ask, and ye shall receive; knock, and it shall be opened unto you" (D&C 88:63).

"For I know the thoughts that I think toward you, saith the Lord, thoughts of peace, and not of evil, . . .

"Then shall ye call upon me, and ye shall go and pray unto me, and I will hearken unto you.

"And ye shall seek me, and find me, when ye shall search for me with all your heart.

"And I will be found of you, saith the Lord" (Jeremiah 29:11–14).

And there are more, many more! So how do we resolve this seeming paradox? We're commanded to pray, urged to pray, encouraged to pray, and promised absolutely that prayer will give us what we seek. The scriptures are full of miracles about answered prayers; but our personal lives, even though they contain examples of answered prayers, often give us painful examples of seemingly unanswered prayers or postponed answers. Are we being told two things when only one of them can be true? I think one of the answers may lie in what I call sparrow prayers.

Sparrow prayers are the little prayers that the Lord can answer when granting our request to the great prayers is not possible. Despite our faithfulness, the Lord may not reverse the course of a crippling cancer that is slowly taking the life of a beloved mother or brother. But he may be able to grant a prayer for a good night's sleep or a pain-free afternoon. He may not grant the prayer of a righteous woman for marriage, but he may teach her the very real pleasures of solitude and give her other companions who are also valiant and honorable.

I think we are surrounded by angels who are anxious to help

us, to breathe comfort and consolation when we are sorrowing and anguished. They do not desert us when we have bitter moments or angry moments, and their companionship and that of the Holy Ghost may be the truest answer to our prayers when we ask those terrible questions without an answer—those questions of "Why?" and "Why me?" and "Is this what obedience brings?" Just because mortality does not provide answers does not mean that eternity lacks answers. And it is only when we fail to find answers in one place—fail but without being punished or reproached—that we can turn to other places.

I also believe that part of our responsibility is to develop a maturity of perspective so that as we struggle with the difficult questions of "why?" we can see deeper reasons. A poem found on the body of a Confederate soldier during the U. S. Civil War addresses this aspect of unanswered prayer.

> I asked for strength that I might achieve.
> He made me weak that I might obey.
> I asked for health that I might do greater things.
> I was given grace that I might do better things.
> I asked for riches that I might be happy.
> I was given poverty that I might be wise.
> I asked for power that I might have the praise of men.
> I was given weakness that I might feel the need of God.
> I asked for all things that I might enjoy life.
> I was given life that I might enjoy all things.
> I received nothing that I asked for.
> All that I hoped for.
> My prayer was answered.[1]

This brings me to my second point—the necessity of trusting the Lord and having faith where we lack knowledge. We came into this world to learn to walk by faith, to learn to choose good rather than evil, not on the basis of immediate rewards, but on the long-term basis of love for goodness itself and love for God who is our Father and for his Son who is our Savior.

In other words, what we are trying to build is a relationship, not just a repertoire of magic words or scientific formulas. When we have faith, it means that we trust the relationship that we have. We trust that God loves us even when hard and painful things happen to us. It means that we trust Jesus to be with us even when we feel most abandoned. It means that we have faith that it is better to act with honesty and integrity, even when we are surrounded by liars and cheaters, that it is better to behave with kindness even when we receive harshness, and that it is better to serve others than to exploit them.

The scriptures assure us: "All things work together for good to them that love God" (Romans 8:28). Faith over the long haul teaches us that this is true.

Psalm 84:3 says: "Yea, the sparrow hath found an house, and the swallow a nest for herself, where she may lay her young, even thine altars, O Lord of hosts, my King, and my God." I love thinking of these little birds, valuable only to the Lord, who has each one of them numbered and counted to him, nesting in safety and trust on the altar of the Lord of hosts and King of kings. That's the kind of relationship we need to carry us through those terrible times when our prayers are not answered according to our desires.

Examples of Sparrow Prayers

A friend gave me a little poster that reads: "When you are dealing with a difficult person, don't let your eyes roll upward. If you need to pray, please be more subtle."

I thought of this when I heard the story about the harried

bishop's wife who had invited dinner guests home from church and had had a pretty frazzled day between planning a menu that could cook while they were gone, getting her children ready for church, sitting through the meetings, getting everyone home, making the final dinner preparations, greeting her guests, and getting the food on the table when her bishop-husband finally got there. The husband asked their four-year-old daughter to ask the blessing. The four-year-old was feeling fractious and whined, "I don't know what to say. What should I say?" The father knew she was showing off for the company, but he just said mildly, "Just say what you've heard Mommy say." So the four-year-old bowed her head and said, "Oh, Lord, why did I ever invite all these people for dinner?"

Well, these are just two examples to get us to think in a lighter mood about prayer, because it's been my experience that sparrow prayers are delightful surprises, happy little "I love you" messages from God. And since one of their characteristics is that they're not the kind of answers that finds a cure for cancer or stops a war, they're always astonishing because they didn't *have* to be answered. So they're also always characterized by pure grace and love. They're unbirthday presents. They're surprise packages.

Such answers teach us not to take ourselves too seriously. Marian Wright Edelman, who is a wonderful and impressive advocate for children in the United States, has a little prayer that we could all use to remind us not to take ourselves too seriously. She says: "Lord, I want to be free of the pressure to do great things in the world by being great in doing small things for Thee."[2]

All God wants is for us to do what we can. He wants us to say "yes" to the small things, and then he promises to make them great. Consider the story of a schoolteacher named Jeanine Greenhaw Waterworth. Her mother was ill and getting worse. Jeanine felt that God wasn't hearing her prayers and that he didn't care about her mother. You can imagine how she felt. Then something wonderful happened. She taught in a private Christian school. It was a glorious fall day and the meetinghouse in which they held classes stood on ten acres forested with beautiful oaks that had carpeted the ground two feet thick with leaves. All of her students were so anxious to get out among them for recess, especially Barry, who had a new watch—an unbelievable treasure for a little black boy. He announced that he would keep track of their extra-long recess that day and was the leader in the games as they whooped and hollered and ran and tumbled over what seemed like the entire ten acres. Then, suddenly, Barry noticed that his watch was gone. This is what Jeanine says happened next:

"Miss Greenhaw, I want to pray for my watch," he stated resolutely. "God will help us find it."

I studied Barry's face, my mind whirling with conflicting emotions. I had just finished a series of Bible lessons with my students on the power of prayer. Did I believe what I had taught? I wanted to encourage Barry. I wanted to say to him, "Yes, let's pray, and God will hear you." But I pictured Barry and the other children wandering around in those 10 acres of dead leaves, waiting for God to answer an impossible prayer.

I started to open my mouth to protest, but Barry had already dropped to his knees. "Dear Jesus," I heard him say with childish sincerity. "I lost my watch, and I know You know where it is. It's the best one I've ever had. Could You please help me find it? Thanks! Amen."

The "amen" was barely out of his mouth when Barry jumped up and ran toward the back hill. Halfway up the hill, he bent down, picked up an object, and let out another whoop. "I found it! It was right here under these leaves."

Barry and the other children danced around the spot, laughing and chattering. Then he examined his watch more closely.

"Oh no," he groaned. "Now I see why it fell off. It's still buckled, but the pin is gone. Now we have to ask Jesus to help us find the pin."

As thrilled as I was at what had obviously been an answer to Barry's prayer, this was just too much. A watch is one thing, but to expect to find a tiny gold pin in knee-deep oak leaves was preposterous. I was about to tell Barry so, but he was already on his knees again. When I heard his "amen," I started for the little group.

I had taken five steps through the leaves, when suddenly a ray of sunlight glinted on something tiny and golden, resting—as if waiting for me—on a huge oak leaf. I gulped and my heart pounded as I reached over and picked it up. It was the pin to Barry's watch.[3]

You see, Barry was right. The Lord *did* know where the watch was, and he also knew where the pin was. Why could he answer those prayers when Jeanine's prayers about her mother's suffering were not being answered? I don't know, but the answer to Barry's prayer was also a comfort to Jeanine.

Many of you have heard about Dr. Larry Dossey. Dr. Dossey was doing his residency in Dallas when he had his first cancer patient, a man with cancer that had spread through both lungs. He had few treatment options and decided not to treat his cancer aggressively, yet every time Dr. Dossey stopped by his room, the sick man was surrounded with visitors from his church, singing and praying. A year later when he was working at another hospital, a colleague casually told him that the man was still alive and asked if he wanted to see his chest X-rays. They were completely clear. There was no sign of cancer. But he had received no treatment—unless you counted prayer. Dr. Dossey didn't know how to explain it.

Many years later, Dr. Dossey came across a rigid, double-blind study that had been done by a cardiologist at San Francisco General Hospital. Half of a group of cardiac patients were prayed for and half were not. Those who were did significantly better. But neither the patients, nurses, nor doctors knew which group the patients were in. It stunned Dr. Dossey. He said, "If the technique being studied had been a new drug or a surgical procedure instead of prayer, it would have been heralded as some sort of breakthrough."

He began looking for other studies on the effect of prayer in treating illness and found more than one hundred experiments that met scientific standards. Now he researches the connection between prayer and health full-time. He has come to six conclusions:

1. The power of prayer does not diminish with distance and exists outside of time. It is just as effective to pray for someone thousands of miles away as it is to pray for someone at their bedside.

2. Prayer can be continuous. To a prayerful person, an

attitude of prayerfulness can continue even when the person is doing other activities or even while he or she is asleep. He quoted a spiritual leader called Isaac the Syrian who said, "When the Spirit has come to reside in someone, that person cannot stop praying; for the spirit prays without ceasing in him."

3. There is no right or wrong way to address God. You can say a memorized prayer or pray spontaneously, although apparently those who offer personalized prayers don't give up as quickly.

4. The best kind of prayer is not a specific list of instructions to God but a prayer that leaves the method of achieving the result up to God. Dr. Dossey pointed out that it can be quite bewildering, in dealing with a specific health problem, to know whether you should pray for an increase or decrease of blood flow to a specific organ, for an increase or a decrease in a specific type of blood cell. Prayers of relinquishment, such as "thy will be done" may seem like giving up to some people, but they actually seem to work best.

5. Love increases the power of prayer. He told about the tangible power of this love. One survey of 10,000 men with heart disease found a 50 percent reduction in frequency of chest pain among married men who perceived their wives as supportive and loving.

And then he told the story about a boy who nursed a wounded pigeon back to health and gave it an identification tag. The next winter, the boy became ill and was rushed to a hospital two hundred miles away. While he was recovering, a pigeon tapped at the window and, when a nurse opened it, flew in. It was the boy's pigeon, the identification tag still in place. The bird had never been to this place before.

And this story led to Dr. Dossey's sixth characteristic of prayer:

6. Prayer reminds us that we are not alone and connects us to "that part of us that is infinite in space and time."[4]

All of this tells us what we already know. Never underestimate the power of your sparrow prayers. Never underestimate the power of your willingness to say "yes" to the Lord, leaving the ways and the means up to him.

Conclusion

Almost certainly the next time you go outside, you will see a sparrow. When you do, I want you to raise your heart in thanksgiving to the Lord. I want you to remember that the Lord's eye is on that sparrow, and the Lord's eye is on you, too. Remember that the Lord's love is unfailing. He wants our happiness, and he wants our growth. Seemingly unanswered prayers may seem to be a cruel betrayal of our most deeply cherished hopes, but they are an opportunity for us to trust in the Lord and to manifest our faith in that relationship.

Nest in safety on the altar of the living God, the Lord of hosts, you and your little ones. His eye is on the sparrow. The hairs of your head are numbered.

For us, as for the Nephites, will come a time when "the mourning, and the weeping, and the wailing . . . did cease; and their mourning was turned into joy, and their lamentations into the praise and thanksgiving unto the Lord Jesus Christ, their Redeemer" (3 Nephi 10:10).

It is my faith that the Lord loves us. He will not leave us comfortless. He will not abandon us. He will be with us in the deep waters of our lives and the deserts and our wilderness, and in him we may safely trust.

NOTES

1. "Unanswered Prayer," *The Plain Truth*, Introductory Issue (no date), 28.

2. Marian Wright Edelman, *Guide My Feet: Prayers and Meditations on Loving and Working for Children* (Boston: Beacon Press, 1995), 66.

3. Jeanine Greenhaw Waterworth, as told to JoAnne Chitwood Collier, "Barry's Watch," *Signs of the Times* 121, no. 10 (n.d.), 30–31.

4. Larry Dossey, "When Science Investigates Prayer," *Guideposts*, June 1995, 37–39.

10

THE BLESSINGS OF SISTERHOOD

ometimes, when I'm speaking to a congregation of sisters, I ask how many of them were born to parents who were members of the Church and how many made the decision to convert to Mormonism. (Some of them aren't sure what to answer until I explain that it's not a trick question and that I'm not going to say, "Aha! What's wrong with the rest of you? We should all be converts!")

It gives us, as a group, a common body of information upon which to talk about choices. Obviously, they made choices that day to be present instead of being somewhere else; and for many women that decision involved making some fairly complicated arrangements about other pieces of their lives that needed to be taken care of. It's a choice that I appreciate very much, as you can imagine. The second point I like to make is that we come from many different backgrounds and different directions to form the group that we are in. Our diversity is one of our greatest strengths and one of the sources of our unity as Mormon women. And my third point is that our sisterhood rests on the strong and unshakable foundation of Christ's love.

Choice

Our right to choose is eternal. We sometimes say that it is God-given, but even that is not completely accurate. It is God-*protected*, but the right to choose is part of our eternal being. God cannot and will not take that right away from us, or he would cease to be God. It is Satan who sought to take away our agency in the premortal existence, and it is still Satan who tries to take away our agency here. If you are getting messages from any quadrant that say, "We will make the decisions for you" or "Just do what we say," I hope little warning bells go off to say, "Why am I getting this message?" and "What will the results be if I let someone else make this decision for me?"

I also hope that we will be equally careful about *giving* those messages. I realize that there's an enormous temptation when we're dealing with our children to say, "I know better than you. Do it my way or else!" But if we do it with our children, then I think it's easy to find ourselves also doing it with sisters who are less experienced in the Church or less experienced in their callings. As Elder M. Russell Ballard has made so clear in his general conference talks and books, the proper order of a council is to be sure every member has a voice and that his or her concerns are listened to and understood; then when the decision is made, even if it is different from the decision we might prefer, we can sustain it.

So this is the first point I want to make. Choose to participate, to contribute, and to belong. Don't be observers. Don't be silent. Don't be timid shadows on the outskirts of the Relief Society program or shy hangers-on closest to the doorways in the Relief Society rooms.

I hope we can find ways for all of the voices and all of the experiences to be heard and talked about in the sisterly circle of Relief Society. I hope there won't be unanswered questions that some sisters won't dare ask out of fear that only the women who have been in the Church for a very long time have the right to participate. I hope there won't be a feeling that the individual experiences and thoughts of some sisters are less important than those of others.

The Lord has made this beautiful and appealing promise: "For it shall come to pass in that day, that every man shall hear the fulness of the gospel in his own tongue, and in his own language, through those who are ordained unto this power, by the administration of the Comforter, shed forth upon them for the revelation of Jesus Christ" (D&C 90:11).

What does it mean to hear the fulness of the gospel in your own language? I thought of this scripture when I was in England and trying to remember that I needed to look for taxis and buses coming on the left side of the road and remembering that flats are apartments, not shoes, and that lifts are elevators and not things you put in shoes. I admired the missionaries who had learned to understand and speak this language so that they could communicate the fulness of the gospel in it. I loved the language of England because of what it told me about the people of England. I tried to soak up just as much culture as I could not only because I wanted to learn about it but also because showing respect for a person's national or ethnic background is a way of showing respect for that person. It's a way of saying: "Where you come from and how you do things and how you say things is important to me because *you* are important to me."

One church leader who used this verse as a sermon text made me think more deeply when he said, "I do not think I am treating this text irresponsibly to suggest that we might well include the language of children, of youth, of the poor, of the affluent, of the educated and uneducated, and of any other group whose language is their gateway to hearing and understanding. Although the in-house vocabulary of [Mormonism] may fall easily from our lips, we will do well to remember that such language may serve as a barrier rather than a gateway."[1]

Diversity

The second point on the subject of sisterhood that I want to make is the strength that comes from diversity. I really enjoyed reading letters of children to God. Here's one about racial diversity from a ten-year-old named Andy:

"God, I know a kid at school. His name is Tom Chen. He is Chinese. Most of us are not. Boy you like to have variety. Love, Andy."

And here's a comment from eight-year-old Amanda about ethnic diversity:

"Dear God, I live in Maine. I have a lot of friends here. People here are great. Some people say we talk funny. That makes me mad. They should talk. They are from Boston. Love, Amanda.

"P. S. My mother's friends live in Boston."

And here's an eight-year-old, Linda, who has a question about religious diversity:

"Dear God, Are Hebrew schools better than regular schools? I know that you must be Jewish, but try to be honest."[2]

I know quite a bit about racial and ethnic diversity. I grew up in Hawaii, and I joined the Church as a convert at age fifteen, so I've been a member for more than sixty years—a whole lifetime's worth. Over the years I have encountered many people who convey, sometimes unconsciously but sometimes on purpose, that converts are not quite as good as lifelong members—that they aren't as committed, that they don't understand the gospel as well, that they don't take the gospel as seriously, and that they still have something to prove before they can be fully accepted. Perhaps it's not necessary to say that I'm very sorry for people who have this perspective. I think it's true that the lifelong members of the Church may sometimes have an immense advantage in having been born and reared inside the culture of the particular ethnic group that we call Mormonism. They know how to pray using Mormon language. They know almost instinctively how to find their way around a meetinghouse. They easily use terms like CTR and PPI. There *is* great strength in the security of knowing a system from the inside out.

But there is also an inherent weakness in being an insider. It means that you may not be a good interpreter when it's necessary to interface with a group outside the Church. We literally don't know the language of another group. We don't know what their customs are. We may be willing to pray with them, but we are surprised if they stand up to pray or if they use different prayer language than we do. These differences are not hard to bridge; but someone who has no experience in making these necessary cultural translations may feel uneasy and even affronted by these differences, rather than accepting them as natural and normal. And, meanwhile, people in the other group may be feeling uneasy and uncomfortable with Latter-day Saint language and customs. What a blessing, in these situations, to have a sister convert who has roots in that other religious tradition or is connected to the outside group in some way and can easily provide interpretation.

And certainly we should seek to build these bridges, to be flexible and understanding. The great blessing that comes to us through the growth of the Church makes it clear that all members everywhere need to be prepared to communicate respectfully and clearly to many different kinds of religious and community groups.

Can you understand why I see diversity as a great strength, enabling us to learn from each other? Carolyn Rasmus, the former executive assistant to the Young Women general board, and a convert herself, points out: "[We are] a diverse church made up of people with unique and different backgrounds. We represent a diversity in age, experiences, talents, family and personal situations, languages spoken and understood, education, marital status, and church callings. But more important than our diversity are the things that bind us together and unite us. For all of our diversity, we are united by our bond of faith in the Lord Jesus Christ and in our commitment to The Church of Jesus Christ of Latter-day Saints. We are people of faith. It is the thing which sets us apart from the world. It is what makes us brothers and sisters in the fullest sense of the word. Faith is the unifying factor that created a common bond between me and . . . sisters around the world, with our next door neighbors or with the person seated beside or behind or in front of you. We are sisters and brothers of a common faith. It is our faith, I believe, that not only brings us together but which will in the end be the only thing that really matters."[3]

I know you have been touched, as I have, by the sincerity and faith of President Gordon B. Hinckley in saying that there is a place for each of us in the Church. He says, "Every morning when I kneel before the Lord in prayer I thank Him for the faithful people of this Church. I am very sincere about that. We are members of The Church of Jesus Christ of Latter-day

Saints, and that bonds us in a brotherhood and sisterhood that is sweet and marvelous and wonderful."[4]

President Hinckley is concerned about retention and fellowshipping. He feels keenly the loss of members who do not feel at home in the Church and who slip out of activity for one reason or another. That suggests that we should have lots of understanding and no harsh judgments for people who temporarily don't want to be at church with us. I believe that most of them will eventually respond to our acceptance.

I think we should make it easier for people to stay active by providing sincere friendship, harder for people to slip away by making it clear how much we respect each individual and how much we need the contributions of each individual, and also much, much easier for people to come back by not judging them or making them feel guilty or inadequate as they end a period of inactivity.

Elder Robert E. Sackley tells the story about a fellow school administrator, also known as a prominent Mormon hater, who extended many invitations to Elder Sackley to go fishing with him. When at last Elder Sackley had an afternoon free, the two men went out in a boat together. There, as they sat placidly casting their lines into the lake and waiting for a bite, the man confided that he had once been a Latter-day Saint but, because he felt that other members had been unfair to him over the years, he had disassociated himself. Elder Sackley, he said, was the only Latter-day Saint he had any respect for or felt he could trust.

Distressed by these comments, Elder Sackley paid a visit to his friend's home that evening. When the man found out Elder Sackley wanted to discuss the Church, he ordered him to leave.

"You opened the discussion yourself this afternoon," Elder Sackley told him, "and I'm not leaving until you hear me out. I love you," he continued. "I know without question that the Church is true and that you've made a shocking mistake with your own life. You've been driven out of the Church by your own foolishness and Word of Wisdom problems." The conversation continued, with neither man budging an inch. Finally, believing he had done all he could, yet reaffirming his faith in their friendship, Elder Sackley went home. Both men were shaken and unsettled.

Several hours later, Elder Sackley was awakened by a telephone call from his friend. Through contrite tears, the man confessed he had been unable to sleep and asked Elder Sackley to please come back. They talked through the night, but this time the conversation was different, as the bitter, unrelenting shackles gradually began to soften and melt away from the friend's long-troubled heart.

"As he struggled to return from thirty-five years of inactivity, he experienced some of the most terrible fear I've ever seen a man go through," Elder Sackley said. "He was afraid that if he went back to Church the building would fall on him or that people would smell cigarette smoke on his clothes and mock or rebuff him. I told him I would handle anyone who did that." Together the two friends went to church. Not many months later his friend was sealed to his wife in the House of the Lord, and Elder Sackley was a witness.

An additional chapter of the story began twelve years later with another phone call. The Sackleys had since moved 450 miles away to Edmonton, and the call was from the man's wife, who told him her husband was dying of lung cancer, a victim of the cigarette habit he had kicked years earlier. He had asked her to call his old friend. The next day Elder Sackley stood by the hospital bedside of his friend, who said, "I want to tell you something I've never told another man. I love you." He then requested that Elder Sackley speak at his funeral and "tell all of my rowdy friends to repent and change their lives." He had one more request: "I'm pretty sure you're going to make it to the celestial kingdom, but I'm not too certain about me. If I make it, will you look me up? I'd like to know we will meet on the other side."

Elder Sackley promised, and the men embraced. Three days later another call brought the news that his friend had died. "I loved that man," he says, then adds, with a twinkle in his eye, "We'll see each other again. We have an appointment to go home teaching together in heaven."[5]

As I think about the beautiful sisterhood of women in the Church, my heart leaps up because I feel the love of the Savior linking us together in a relationship that truly is a foretaste of the association we will have in heaven.

But we can have more moments like this on earth. I hope that each week in Relief Society, or even chance encounters at the grocery store, will bring the same lift of the heart and the same recognition of sisterhood.

Sisterhood

In addition to the importance of choosing to participate and the need for diversity, let me share a thought or two on strengthening our sisterhood. This isn't a recipe book list of "how-to's." I want to start by reviewing with you why sisterhood is possible at all. It's because of Jesus. I testify with the Apostle Paul that "neither death, nor life, nor angels, nor principalities, nor powers, nor things present, nor things to come, nor height, nor depth, nor any other creature, shall be able to separate us from the love of God, which is in Christ Jesus our Lord" (Romans 8:38–39).

That love is total. It is complete. It is perfect. But we are not perfect, and we do not live in a world that is perfect. Our families are not perfect. *We* are not perfect. Our wards and stakes are not perfect. Our understanding of the gospel is not perfect, and, for sure, our *living* of the gospel is not perfect. Part of our task in mortality is to deal with that imperfection in exactly the same way that our Savior deals with *our* imperfections: by becoming perfect in love. As the Apostle Peter testified: "Above all things have fervent charity among yourselves: for charity shall cover the multitude of sins" (1 Peter 4:8).

As sisters, I ask you in all soberness and sincerity to reflect on these three questions:

First, do you know, as the Apostle Paul did, that nothing, nothing at all, can separate you from the love of Jesus? If you do not, I suspect that it is not because you don't want to know but because you think that somehow you are not worthy of his love. Please believe me: The Savior does not require your perfection. What he asks you to give him is "a broken heart and a contrite spirit" (2 Nephi 2:7). He told the Prophet Joseph Smith: "Behold, the Lord requireth the heart and a willing mind" (D&C 64:34).

I implore you to go on your knees and ask with the simplicity of a child: "Please tell me that you love me. Please let me feel your love." Don't let fears and worries and apologies for your sins and imperfections drown out the still small voice so that it can't answer you. I promise you that you will sing, with Bernard of Clairvaux: "Jesus, the very thought of thee, with sweetness fills my breast" (*Hymns*, no. 141).

Now, if you don't have an answer to this first question like fire in your bones, don't worry about the second and third questions yet. That would be like pouring the cake batter in the pans without mixing it up first. I'm serious. Until our relationship with Jesus and Heavenly Father is right, there isn't even a good way to answer the second and third questions.

The second question is this: Knowing what you do about the Savior and our Heavenly Father and their inexhaustible love for you, and yours for them, and because you have made sacred covenants at the waters of baptism, at the sacrament table, and in the temple with them, is there *anything* that anyone can do to separate you from this church, which contains the true gospel of Jesus Christ, the power of the priesthood, and the ordinances of salvation? Can anyone hurt your feelings or ignore your opinions or shun you socially in any way that will make you turn away from the Church?

If you don't know that Jesus is the Christ and your Savior, and if you don't know that Heavenly Father lives and loves you, then for you the main point of your membership in the Church is basically to meet social and service needs, and you could probably do that just as well through another church or through the PTA or through the Junior League or the local historical society.

But if you know that God lives and loves you and wants you to be in his church, then you can accept the imperfections of other members because you know why the Church exists and that your covenant is with a community as well as with your Savior and your Heavenly Father. Now, please understand that I'm not saying that you should put up with bullying and unfairness. Bullies need to repent, and insensitive people need to develop sensitivity or they won't be able to grow spiritually. But stay close to the Lord so that you can separate the real imperfections of the people in your ward from the beauty and holiness of the Church that contains the priesthood ordinances of salvation. Elder Sackley said: "I have only one reason for being a member of the Church. When I heard the gospel, it struck me like a thunderbolt. I am totally convinced of its truthfulness."[6]

Now, if you've considered the first question, and the answer is yes—nothing can separate you from the love of Jesus, and the answer to the second question is no—there is nothing anyone can do to force you away from the Church—then perhaps the third question is the most important of all. Sisters, I ask you to consider with great humility this question: "If you are founded and grounded in the Savior's love and if nothing anyone else might do can possibly force you away from the Church, then is there anything *you* are doing that is making it harder for someone to come to church or to be at church with you?"

For example, do you find yourself tuning out some women who have had different experiences from yours? Do you find yourself unwilling to learn from the adversity that some women have suffered because you have decided they have brought their poverty or their divorce or their wayward children on themselves?

If you're a leader, do you talk to everyone and do you listen to everyone? Do you assume that some people are right for certain callings while others just aren't and never will be? Do you think that some people's opinions are sounder or more reliable or more worth listening to than others?

If anything I'm saying brings even a pinprick to your conscience, I implore you to go again on your knees and ask our

Heavenly Father to tell you how he feels about that woman and to permit you to see her the way *he* sees her.

Quoting his father, Mormon, Moroni implores us: "Pray unto the Father with all the energy of heart, that ye may be filled with this love, which he hath bestowed upon all who are true followers of his Son, Jesus Christ; that ye may become the [children] of God; that when he shall appear we shall be like him, for we shall see him as he is" (Moroni 7:48). If we are filled with the love of Christ, we will not only see *him* as he is but we will see *others* as he sees them. I promise you that barriers of separation within your heart that are holding your sisters at a distance will crumble. They will disappear even in the moment when you realize, in the sacred presence of our Savior, that they exist.

Conclusion

Let's build our sisterhood by building on our firm and unshakable testimonies in the love of Jesus Christ and our Heavenly Father. Let's take responsibility into our own hands for *belonging* to the Church and for making sure that it belongs to us—that no one can drive us away or take it away from us. And with those two cornerstones, then perhaps we can see what we may be doing that makes it harder for others to stay attached, and with great joy and gratitude we can repent so that our circle of sisterhood will remain unbroken.

Sisters, may the blessings of our Lord and Savior Jesus Christ shower down upon you, that you will feel the swelling in your heart and spirit that answers his own boundless mercy and his own joy with each enlargement of ourselves that we make so that we can better contain his perfection. And as sisters, I pray for us an increase of love, of hope, of happiness, of humility, and of joy.

NOTES

1. Geoffrey Spencer, "Put Out into the Deep!" *Saints Herald,* June 1992, 8.

2. David Heller, *Dear God* (New York: Berkeley Publishing Group, 1987), 29, 32, 52.

3. Carolyn J. Rasmus, "The Faithful Heritage of a Convert," in *A Heritage of Faith: Talks Selected from the BYU Women's Conferences,* edited by Mary E. Stovall and Carol Cornwall Madsen (Salt Lake City: Deseret Book Co., 1988), 40–41.

4. "Messages of Inspiration from President Hinckley," *Church News,* 1 June 1996, 1.

5. Derin Head Rodriguez, *From Every Nation* (Salt Lake City: Deseret Book Co., 1990), 184–86.

6. Ibid., 186.

11

Inner Peace

e are not the "Glamour-day Saints" or the "Someday
Something Special-day Saints" but we are the "Latter-day
Saints." And when are the latter days? They're right now,
today. Our job is to be holy and to find holiness in what happens on Monday and Tuesday as well as what happens on
Sunday. Then we can experience peace. We can be at peace
with ourselves and with this world God has given us, and we
can bring peace to others.

Let's consider two ways we can build this sense of sacred-
ness into our daily lives. The first is to trust—to have confidence in ourselves. And the second way is to trust in the Lord.

Confidence in Ourselves

What is the relationship between confidence and holiness?
We could call that relationship faith. If we are afraid, we cannot love, but we all know that perfect love casteth out fear. A
wise teacher, Soetsu Yanagi, observed, "Even the common
articles made for daily use become endowed with beauty when
they are loved."[1] Even though housecleaning is hard work, isn't
there a moment when the light that winks from shining sur-
faces mirrors love and says, "This is a good place to be"? Of

course, we want our homes to be comfortable and welcoming for our families; but this end, desirable though it is, does not recognize that the process of cleaning and cooking and making beds is a way of communicating with gentle, loving touches: "Be the best you can be. Do the best you can." It's as loving to tend a house, a garden, a work-space, or a classroom as it is to tend a child or an aging grandparent or a marriage.

And it doesn't happen without strength and competence. There is no question that the Saints of today need to be strong and capable. We need to develop our resources and use them wisely. When Presidency Gordon B. Hinckley spoke at the Weber State Institute, he was asked what trait he admired most in Sister Hinckley, and he said, "Endurance!" Endurance is something we also admire in our pioneer forebears. As we contemplate the strength and devotion of those courageous souls, we are grateful to have those traits as part of our heritage. I enjoyed a newspaper column by Sharon Randall that described some of the reasons we need strength. She wrote: "Recently my daughter suggested that I should get a life. . . . Get a life? I beg your pardon? You can accuse me of all sorts of things, but don't try to tell me I don't have a life. I have more life than I know what to do with.

"I've got a full-time job and a family (a husband, three not-yet-grown children and a neurotic dog), a house that defies order, a yard that deserves Agent Orange. I even have friends whose names I recall occasionally. If I had more life I'd be dead."

Then Sharon remembered her own eighteenth summer when she thought her own mother needed a life.

"I told [my mother] I thought she ought to get out more often, do something interesting, have a little fun.

"'My life is about as interesting as I can stand,' she said.

'I work Monday through Friday, clean my house on Saturday, see my mother every Sunday rain or shine. I don't need fun. I need help.'"[2]

Well, is there a little something in that story that most of us can relate to—men as well as women? Where does the strength come from when we need it? I want to suggest that if knowledge is power—and as an educator, I truly believe that it is—then one of the most important pieces of knowledge we can have is self-knowledge. Yet there are powerful forces that work against self-knowledge. We are flooded with experience. We are busy from morning to night. But what does our experience mean? What significance do our choices have? Can we see them connecting us to the sacred? Do they speak to our eternal selves?

Parker Palmer, a philosopher and educator whom I admire very much, tells the story of a man who came to see Carl Jung, the famous psychologist, for help because he was depressed.

"Jung told him to cut back his fourteen-hour workday to eight, go directly home after work, and spend the evenings in his study, quiet and all alone. So the man tried. He went to his study, shut the door, read a little Hesse or Mann, played a few Chopin études or some Mozart. After some weeks of this he returned to Jung complaining that he could see no improvement. On learning how the man had spent his time Jung said, 'But you didn't understand. I didn't want you to be with Hesse or Mozart or Mann or Chopin. I wanted you to be all alone with yourself.' The man looked terrified and exclaimed, 'I can't think of any worse company.' Jung replied, 'Yet this is the self you inflict on other people fourteen hours a day' (and Jung might have added, the self you inflict on yourself all the time)."[3]

Now, how on earth does someone like that learn to like himself a little better? And what is the message that his depression is giving him? Jung's patient was drugging himself with overwork to avoid facing himself. Many of us are doing exactly the same thing, plus abusing prescription drugs, plus indulging in other self-abusive and addictive behaviors because we really don't like ourselves very much.

Please don't misunderstand. I am certainly not claiming that no one should ever need therapy or take anti-depressants if they have the gospel. I understand completely that Mormon men and women, just like men and women everywhere, experience clinical depression, discouragement, and bad days ranging all the way from tears and disappointments to suicidal thoughts. This is the real world, and we have to deal with real problems. Nobody is ever rich enough or smart enough or spiritual enough to never have any problems.

What we do have—what the gospel promises us—is that we do not have to be alone and we don't have to be fakes. No matter what the problem is, we should have each other and we have God. Charles H. Spurgeon, the great Christian revivalist, bore his testimony: "As sure as ever God puts his children in the furnace he will be in the furnace with them."[4] I'm not sure I agree that God puts us in the furnace. I think mortality and our own bad decisions, and the bad decisions of others, put us in that furnace. After all, as someone once commented, "Never attribute to evil what can be adequately explained by stupidity." Learning not to be stupid has to be one of the most valuable lessons mortality can bring us. But yes, God will be with us in the furnace.

One pretty wise thirty-something, asked about the greatest lesson [she] had learned in her life so far, said, "I've learned that the prayer I say most often is, 'Lord, please keep your arm around my shoulder and your hand over my mouth.'"[5]

I have a few suggestions for liking ourselves better.

First, lighten up! Ease off! Back up! Lots of us would call the SPCA if someone were to treat the family dog the way we treat ourselves. I can't imagine real Saints fretting, rushing, dithering, or dawdling. Instead of making a job list as long as your leg, lower your expectations. Make a list that contains only half of what you think needs to be done every day. That way, if you finish everything on the list, you can feel pleased. And if you have time to do more, then you can really pat yourself on the back.

Second, enjoy each job. Even routine jobs have pleasant parts to them. Don't wipe down the counter while you're mentally making a list of the three phone calls you need to make next. Really enjoy how clean the counter looks and how tidily you brushed all of those crumbs into your hand. George Washington Carver once said, "If you love it enough, anything will talk with you."[6] I'm sure that loving attentiveness was what led to his success with the peanut.

Sue Bender, a California writer, wrote a book called *Everyday Sacred* in which she talks about her son David, who is a teacher of holiness to her. How? By the way he takes care of his pick-up truck.

"David's truck is ten years old; he's had it for four years and it looks brand new. He cleans it once a week, inside and out, and by the unhurried way he washes the truck, it's clear that he enjoys this routine. . . .

"'Watching you wash your truck,' I told David, 'I felt I was witnessing an act of devotion, certainly not a chore.'

"'I'm not sure what devotion means,' he said, shaking his

head, 'but I do think it sort of reflects that my business is in order when I have a clean, well-conditioned truck. It says something about me.'

"David's connection with his truck, his sense of peace and attention, the way he has of caring for the things he uses, made me think of a line from the poet Rilke:

" 'When a poet rubs a piece of furniture,' Rilke said, 'when he puts a little fragrant wax on his table with the woolen cloth, he registers this object officially as a member of the human household.'"[7]

Third, if you have a job where you don't need to be talking or thinking about it, sing while you work. If we're supposed to hum a hymn to crowd a temptation out of our thoughts, then why not try the same thing when you're trying to bring more sunshine into your life?

Fourth, reward yourself for every job you get done. Remember in Genesis when God was creating the heavens and the earth? From the Book of Moses, we know that God the Father, Jehovah, Michael, and others were involved in this great creative effort, the culmination of a long process that had begun with spiritual creation. And after every step, what did these creators do? Did they say, "Good grief, the creation of the butterflies took ten minutes longer than we had planned. Put on a burst of speed on the whales. And you're grounded tonight until you're sure that those sunflowers are all going to turn their heads to follow the sun." No, they didn't beat themselves or each other up. And they didn't instantly plunge into the next task. They enjoyed the accomplishment. "And God saw that it was good." When we have accomplished something worthwhile, we need to savor that accomplishment.

Fifth, have some priorities that distinguish between "nice," "important" and "essential." Some things are important but not essential. In other words, they're not worth doing in themselves—because they're not all that creative or wonderful or fun or significant per se—but because the consequences of neglecting them are unpleasant. I refer to the laundry, for instance. Nobody would write down on their list of goals when they graduate from high school that in five years they want to do the laundry. It's important, but it's not essential. What's essential are the principles of cleanliness, helpfulness, and self-reliance.

On tasks such as this, tasks that are necessary because there are unpleasant consequences if they don't get done, I think you should be very generous about sharing both the responsibility and the consequences. Most children by the age of eight can sort light and dark clothes, put them in the washing machine, measure the detergent, and push the right buttons. Maybe they'll need to climb on a step stool for part of that job, but they can do it. Why should the parents be the laundry monarchs of the house? Similarly, if you work with someone who is used to slacking off because you have always been willing to pick up the slack, maybe you should be sure that the consequences follow the performance. It may feel very important to you to be liked, but it's essential for you to also keep your self-respect.

Maybe some of you are always patient, always sweet, and deal with hurt feelings in private and, as a result, you are the safest person in your family or your office to get mad at when something goes wrong. One woman's married daughter does this after her husband has yelled at her. She never confronts her husband about his crummy behavior, but she calls up her mother and quarrels fiercely with her, no matter what her mother says. It's because she doesn't feel safe with her husband but feels safe with her mother. Still, it's not a good thing for their relationship. It's important for this mother to be kind and patient to her daughter, but it's essential for her to also teach her to be fair. Maybe if the daughter were clearer about being fair to her mother, she could be clearer about not letting her husband be unfair to her.

Sixth, make taking care of yourself one of your highest priorities. Take time for yourself. Schedule time for self-renewal. Anne Morrow Lindbergh said, "If one sets aside time for a business appointment, a trip to the hairdresser, a social engagement, or a shopping expedition, that time is accepted as inviolable. But if one says: I cannot come because that is my hour to be alone, one is considered rude, egotistical, or strange. What a commentary on our civilization, when being alone is considered suspect; when one has to apologize for it; make excuses, hide the fact that one practices it—like a secret vice."[8]

Anne Morrow Lindbergh was a writer. She needed creative time alone to explore what she thought and felt. She had to have time to search for the skills to express those thoughts and feelings. But time alone is crucial to all of us—time to let the chatter and the busy-ness slow down and stop, time to listen to our feelings, to think a whole thought clear to the end, to enter into an unhurried dialogue with our own spirits and with our Heavenly Father through prayer. Every single one of us needs that.

If you feel unhappy with yourself and guilty when you haven't really done anything wrong, and if you're like Jung's client who doesn't want to spend time by himself, then listen to that message from yourself. Don't turn away from the unhappiness. Acknowledge it. Think about it. Pray about it.

And do something about it. There are lots of self-improvement books available for free in the library, plenty of talk shows on the radio or on television, plenty of useful advice in magazines. There are priesthood leaders, trusted friends, professional therapists, and the intelligence and spiritual intuitions that God gave you. You may think that you're important because of what you do for people—that you're important to the world because you take care of your children or your grandchildren, or teach lessons or volunteer at the shelter or take the Boy Scouts on hikes. You may think you count because of the salary you earn and because you provide for your family. Certainly those things are important. But those are jobs, chores, functions. They are things that someone else could do. What's *essential* about you is who you *are*. If you're someone's spouse or parent or friend or teacher, that's a relationship, not a set of tasks. What's essential in that relationship is you, the real you, not just a smoothly functioning job-doer. No one and no thing can make you happy. Only you can do that. And nothing is more essential.

I've really stressed this point about being happy with yourself, making time for yourself, and enjoying being with yourself. I've done it because I think that we don't have strength unless we have the strength from within of knowing ourselves and liking ourselves. A weak person does not feel peaceful. A weak person does not feel holy. That doesn't mean we should ignore our faults and shortcomings, and it doesn't mean that we should have low standards. But it does mean that we need to be the kind of person we like to spend time with. Otherwise, how can we expect anyone else—such as spouses, children, friends, and work colleagues—to want to spend time with us? This is the peace that comes from our strength within.

Trust in the Lord

My second point is going to sound as if it contradicts the first point, and that is that our peace comes from trusting in the Lord. But these two points don't contradict each other. They really don't. The Lord is willing to meet us where we are. He isn't shocked by our weaknesses or offended by them. But he wants us to be strong. He succors us in our weakness so that we *may* become strong, not so that we will stay permanently weak.

The Lord's methods are interesting. He comforts us, but he does not make us comfortable. He always hears us, but he speaks in a still, small voice so that we have to learn to listen. As Elder Spencer J. Condie has said, "Through the instrumentality of the Holy Ghost, His Spirit comforts those who mourn, teaches and testifies to those who thirst for the truth, purifies the brokenhearted who would be clean, and warns of dangers which lie ahead."[9]

Most of all, he will make us strong and free by teaching us the truth. This is not as easy as it sounds. In many ways, we human beings are frightened by the truth. We don't like the truth because it requires us to change, to sacrifice, and to be strong. But when we truly love Jesus, we cannot be satisfied with anything less than the truth. In our own ways, we, like the brother of Jared, cannot be kept outside the veil, and we will truly see the face of the Lord.

I thrilled to Elder F. Enzio Busche's general conference message when he talked about the importance of the truth. He said:

"Enlightened by the Spirit of truth, we will . . . be able to pray for the increased ability to endure truth and not be made angry by it (see 2 Ne. 28:28). In the depth of such a prayer, we may finally be led to that lonesome place where we suddenly see ourselves naked in all soberness. Gone are all the little lies of self-defense. We see ourselves in our vanities and false hopes for carnal security. We are shocked to see our many deficiencies, our lack of gratitude for the smallest things. We are now at that sacred place that seemingly only a few have courage to enter, because this is that horrible place of unquenchable pain in fire and burning. This is that place where true repentance is born. This is that place where the conversion and the rebirth of the soul are happening. . . . This is the place where suddenly the atonement of Christ is understood and embraced. This is the place where suddenly, when commitments have solemnly been established, the soul begins to 'sing the song of redeeming love' and indestructible faith in Christ is born (Alma 5:26)."[10]

There are times for all of us when we do not understand what is happening or why it is happening or what we are supposed to learn from it. Peace seems very far away. This is the time to be completely honest with the Lord in your prayers and trust completely in him. Let me tell you a story about what I mean.

One of the staunch members of the Church in Japan, and one of the earliest members to be baptized after World War II, is Kan Watanabe, who has served in many positions on the branch, ward, district, and stake level. He was baptized in 1950 and served a mission from 1953 to 1955. In 1967, he began working for the Church Translation Department in Tokyo. He has translated for dozens of visiting General Authorities. The Church in Japan would be very different if he were not there. When my husband was president of the Japan Okinawa Mission, we had a humorous saying, "If we can't do it, Watanabe Kan!"

Then in 1967, the Tokyo Stake was to be organized, and men were being considered for positions. Surely Brother Watanabe would be called. He was interviewed. Elders Ezra Taft Benson and Gordon B. Hinckley asked him for suggestions of worthy men who might serve as stake officers. Soon the interviews were over. The next day, before the dedication of the Mormon Pavilion, Elder Benson called Brother Watanabe and said that the new stake organization had been determined, but that Kan was not included. Hearing that, he knelt in humble prayer and decided that he would serve in whatever position the Lord wanted him. That night Elder Benson called again, this time asking Brother Watanabe to come translate for him at the stake priesthood meeting. Brother Watanabe told his wife and five children about his prayer and that he wanted only to set a good example, wherever he was. That night, feeling somewhat disconnected from stake affairs, he went to the meeting. There he was informed that the missions were being divided, and he was to be the new president of the newest mission of the Church.[11] Then he understood why the calling he and everyone else had expected had not come.

So peace from the Lord comes in two ways. It comes as he walks beside us, helping us and encouraging us as we carry our burdens and making the pathway smoother before us so that we will not stumble. In other words, he helps us build our own spiritual strength by acknowledging and honoring our tasks— not by relieving us of those tasks, but by helping us become strong enough to carry them. And the second way he gives us peace is that, when we cannot do more, or when we simply do not understand, or when we feel so exhausted we want to lie down in the snow and go to sleep, he picks us up and his strength becomes our strength. In his arms, we find rest, comfort, acceptance, and knowledge. And then, he gently sets us on our feet again and says, "This is the way. Walk in it with me." In this walk—humbly, undramatically, everyday—we find holiness.

Peace in Every Season

We've talked about finding the peace in ourselves that comes from developing our strengths and liking ourselves and being happy in ourselves, and we've also talked about finding peace by trusting in the Savior. Now let's consider the seasons of our lives and the different needs for peace that we have in these different seasons. We have seasons where we need to rely on the strength of others, but the goal is always to rest enough to regain our strength so we can go on. It is not to find a permanent crutch. And we always need strength from the Lord. We never outgrow the need for his strength.

We always need peace and draw our strength from what brings us peace. But we need to recognize that we have needs for different kinds of strengths for different seasons. I needed different strengths as a fifteen-year-old when I was joining the Church than I did as a young mother or as an elementary school principal or when my husband died. But in each of those seasons, I needed strength, and the strength I gained was added to and grew out of the earlier strengths I had acquired. No matter what age you are or what stage you are at in your life, you can go on from where you are.

A few years ago, I was asked to write a message for the Young Women of a ward in Florida, which would be enclosed in a time capsule. In ten years, the leaders hoped to reunite all of these girls and their teachers, open the time capsule, and see what changes had come with time.

It was an interesting assignment to look ten years into the future. I want to share with you what I wrote to them. I said:

"I am so honored that you would invite a woman in her seventies to pack her hopes and good wishes and faith next to yours in your time capsule where they will season together gently for the next ten years and be opened with surprise and delight and nostalgia and thanksgiving.

"I'm saying right now that I want to be invited to the opening party!

"Now, maybe you think that I won't be around. It's true that none of us knows the future from day to day, but we should plan as though we had all eternity. Because we do!

"Let's talk about that party in ten years. My first wish for you is that you all *will* be here for it. Realistically, the chances are not good. Disease and accident are invisible companions on our life's journey.

"But I believe that we choose our kinds of death somewhat by the kinds of life we choose. If death comes to you in the next ten years, make it seek you out. Do not seek it out by putting yourself in harm's way, by driving recklessly, or by risking your health through an eating disorder, through an addiction, through sexual promiscuity, or through associating with those who find violent solutions to life's problems.

"My second wish for you is that the years that pass will be joyous ones. I hope that these ten years will bring graduation from high school, a good launching or even completion of your secondary education in whatever form you choose, the beginnings of your life work, marriage in the temple to a good man, and perhaps the birth of your first child or children. But realistically, the chances are not very likely that this wish will come 100 percent true for 100 percent of you. Some of you will not marry. Some of you who do marry will not marry happily. Almost certainly, for some of you, these next ten years will bring the death of a parent or a loved one, divorce within your family—whether of your parents, a sibling, or even your own. Perhaps you will be disappointed in your educational plans, or perhaps your career, however well-prepared you are, will simply not materialize according to your hopes.

"But my third wish is one that I know can be realized, and it is also my blessing on you and my prayer for you. It is a blessing that can be realized, whether in this life or the next. It is a fulfillment that you can reach despite illness, despite disillusionment, despite disappointment, and despite your own temporary betrayal of your deepest dreams. It is this: 'That Christ may dwell in your hearts by faith; that ye, being rooted and grounded in love, may be able to comprehend with all saints what is the breadth, and length, and depth, and height; and to know the love of Christ, which passeth knowledge, that ye might be filled with all the fulness of God' (Ephesians 3:17–20).

"I am praying for you and blessing you with the absolute knowledge that Jesus loves you and that your faith in him will be unshaken. I know that this blessing can be realized. In fact, I guarantee it.

"How can I guarantee this blessing to you? I can because it does not depend on us. It is our Savior, Jesus Christ himself, who is the guarantor. *Our* will may falter. *Our* discipline may slip. We may overestimate *our* ability to resist temptation. We will certainly overestimate our ability to be unfailingly kind, unfailingly patient, unfailingly loving. We will fall short of achieving all of these goals perfectly."

But I want to bear here the same testimony that I bore to

those Young Women in Florida. I testify with all the strength God has given me that our weaknesses, our shortcomings—even our downright sins—cannot take our eternal future away from us if we will follow the voice of Jesus whispering, so gently, so penetratingly, so powerfully: "Look unto me in every thought; doubt not, fear not. Behold the wounds which pierced my side, and also the prints of the nails in my hands and feet; be faithful, keep my commandments, and ye shall inherit the kingdom of heaven. . . . I will never leave thee, nor forsake thee" (D&C 6:36–37; Hebrews 13:5).

Life will bruise and even scar us, but it cannot break us because "If God be for us, who can be against us?" (Romans 8:31).

We have no idea how strong our spirits are—those premortal entities that lived in the presence of our Heavenly Parents, who knew Jesus face to face and loved him and worshipped him and trusted him so completely that we willingly followed him when he volunteered to implement the Father's plan. We are not alone, because he is always with us. We are not weak, because he is our strength. We are not in turmoil because we have his peace. With the Apostle Paul, I promise you: "We are more than conquerors through him that loved us. For I am persuaded, that neither death, nor life, nor angels, nor principalities, nor powers, nor things present, nor things to come, nor height, nor depth, nor any other creature, shall be able to separate us from the love of God, which is in Christ Jesus our Lord" (Romans 8:37–39).

He is our light. He is our strength and our song. He is our Lord, now and forever. He loves us eternally. His peace passes all understanding. His strength is available to us. Our strength will grow a thousandfold as we lean on him and learn from him and walk in his ways.

NOTES

1. Quoted in Frederic Brussat and Mary Ann Brussat, eds., *Spiritual Literacy: Reading the Sacred in Everyday Life* (New York: Simon and Schuster, 1996), 41.

2. Sharon Randall, "Cutting the Cord: Get a Life? What I Need, Dear, Is a Life Jacket," *Deseret News*, 15 August 1993, A2.

3. Parker Palmer, "Borne Again: The Monastic Way to Church Renewal," *Weavings*, 8 September 1986), 14.

4. Tony Castle, comp., *The New Book of Christian Quotations* (New York: Crossroads, 1983), 5.

5. In H. Jackson Brown Jr., comp., *Live and Learn and Pass It On*, vol. 2 (Nashville: Rutledge Hill Press, 1955), 27.

6. Quoted in Frederic Brussat and Mary Ann Brussat, eds., *Spiritual Literacy: Reading the Sacred in Everyday Life* , 41.

7. Sue Bender, *Everyday Sacred: A Woman's Journey Home* (New York: HarperCollins Publishers, 1995), 94–95.

8. Anne Morrow Lindbergh, *Gift from the Sea* (New York: Vintage Books, 1977), 50.

9. Spencer J. Condie, "A Mighty Change of Heart," *Ensign*, November 1993, 17.

10. F. Enzio Busche, "Truth Is the Issue," *Ensign*, November 1993, 25–26.

11. "A Man Is Chosen," *Rising Sun*, April 1970, 418–19.

12

A Message from Enoch

*O*ne of the treasures that the Prophet Joseph Smith restored to us in the latter days is additional knowledge about Enoch. Enoch was an ancient prophet who, like the Book of Mormon prophets, saw our times and wept over our sinfulness and foolishness, but there are ways in which his story has a happy ending, at least in part.

The part of Enoch's story that we know best is that he established a city of such righteousness that the Lord came and dwelled among the people there and then took the city to heaven, away from the wickedness of the world. What better example for us in these troubled times: to draw closer to the Savior and withdraw more completely from the wickedness of the world? We need to make our homes and our wards beacons of righteousness, as Enoch's city was in his own time.

Enoch was born six generations after Adam and Eve and just a few generations before Noah. So he grew up knowing something about the violence, wickedness, and evil doings that were so prevalent in his day, for "Satan had great dominion among men, and raged in their hearts" (Moses 6:15).

The voice of the Lord called young Enoch to his mission, and at first he was reluctant, protesting, "[I] am but a lad, and all the people hate me; for I am slow of speech; wherefore am I thy servant?" The Lord repeated his call to him, reminding him, "Behold my Spirit is upon you, . . . and the mountains shall flee before you, and the rivers shall turn from their course; and thou shalt abide in me, and I in you; therefore walk with me" (Moses 6:31, 34). In fact, this promise was literally fulfilled. When Enoch "spake the word of the Lord, . . . the earth trembled, and the mountains fled, even according to his command; and the rivers of water were turned out of their course . . . so powerful was the word of Enoch" (Moses 7:13).

Furthermore, the Lord commanded Enoch to anoint his eyes with clay and then to wash them, promising he would see things that were concealed from the natural eye (Moses 6:35). Later in his ministry, Enoch had a powerful vision, which is described in Moses, chapter 7. He saw many wonderful things, but I'd like to focus on just four elements: First, the Lord talked to Enoch face to face. Second, the Lord wept over the wickedness of his children. Third, Enoch learned that the earth has a soul that is grieved because of that same wickedness. And fourth, it was in circumstances of great wickedness and corruption that the city of Enoch was established.

Face to Face

Let's begin with the first element: that the Lord talked to Enoch face to face. Enoch tells us he was on a journey and had paused to pray when "there came a voice out of heaven, saying—Turn ye, and get ye upon the mount Simeon." As he obeyed and stood upon the mount, he says: "I beheld the heavens open, and I was clothed upon with glory; and I saw the Lord; and he stood before my face, and he talked with me, even as a man talketh one with another, face to face; and he said unto me: Look, and I will show unto thee the world for the space of many generations" (Moses 7:2–4).

We may say, "Well, that applies to prophets. That doesn't apply to ordinary people like us." But think about it for a minute. We also have journeys that our daily work requires us to take. We also can cry out to the Lord as we go about our tasks. We can receive promptings that will take us to holy places, and the Lord can, and will, and wants to answer our questions—perhaps not about the whole world for many generations, but certainly about our own world of responsibilities and stewardship.

Will he appear and talk to us face to face? I certainly think he has that power if he wishes and if we are worthy, for he promised the Prophet Joseph Smith: "Verily, thus saith the Lord: It shall come to pass that every soul who forsaketh his sins and cometh unto me, and calleth on my name, and obeyeth my voice, and keepeth my commandments, shall see my face and know that I am" (D&C 93:1). I have had experiences in prayer—and I suspect that you have, too—when the sense of presence and spiritual power is so great that even the sight of our eyes could not make us feel with any greater certainty that the Lord is there, speaking to us as one person speaks to another. And if you have not had that experience, I promise you that you can have it.

Why did the Lord want to show Enoch "the world for the space of many generations"? It's because Enoch's stewardship as a prophet was to see the judgments that would come upon the people if they did not repent—and, in fact, he saw the destruction of the earth's inhabitants by water at the time of his descendant Noah. None of us has that stewardship and none of us has that responsibility, so we do not need *that* vision. But don't we need vision in every other aspect of our everyday lives?

Suppose we are troubled by the tantrums of our two-year-old or the sulkiness of our eleven-year-old. We don't know if these behaviors are a phase that they will grow out of quickly if we ignore them and provide pleasant alternative activities, or if they represent the beginnings of some serious symptoms that need our prompt intervention. But the Lord knows, and he will help us if we ask.

Suppose there's a situation at work that creates tension and unpleasantness. What is the right way to approach it? Should we speak privately but very candidly to the person or persons who seem to be injecting these attitudes into our workplace? Or is this a time for extra consideration and thoughtfulness to soothe the hidden troubles that are manifesting themselves in these ways? Often, we don't know, but the Lord does, and he will help us if we ask.

Suppose you receive a ward or stake calling that you know will be very taxing but also very rewarding. As you consider your family responsibilities and other commitments, you are uncertain what the costs will be if you say yes and not sure what blessings you may not receive if you explain that this isn't a good time. The Lord will enlighten your mind and clarify your feelings as you pray to him for guidance.

Remember Amulek's counsel: "Cry unto him when ye are in your fields, yea, over all your flocks. [What are your fields? Aren't they the places where you have work to do to earn your living? And aren't our flocks the projects and tasks for which we are responsible?]

"Cry unto him in your houses, yea, over all your household, both morning, mid-day, and evening. [Does this mean that we can pray for our families? It certainly does. And I think it also means that we can pray for our houses themselves—for the safety and order and cleanliness and spirit in our homes.]

"Yea, cry unto him against the power of your enemies.

"Yea, cry unto him against the devil, who is an enemy to all righteousness."

Let me pause here for a moment. I think we can understand praying to be delivered from temptation and from things that will distract us from our righteous endeavors; but I think we are less clear about the instructions to cry against the power of our enemies. We're used to thinking, *Well, there may be people I don't get along with, but they're not exactly my* enemies. It may seem paranoid and defensive to think of ourselves as having enemies. And maybe we don't have personal enemies, even though there are people in the world who feel that disliking someone justifies their being rude or actually dangerous.

I think the most dangerous kind of enemy is not someone who hates you personally or who has a grudge against you personally or who purposefully wants to inflict bodily harm on you, but rather is someone who sees you as a means to an end, as an instrument for their pleasure. What about someone who wants to sell your daughter drugs? He may not even know your daughter's name or anything about her; he just wants her money and does not care what the consequences to her life will be. Is he not your enemy and your daughter's enemy?

President Gordon B. Hinckley has warned us repeatedly about the addictive and destructive nature of pornography. What about the person who wants to sell your husband a filthy magazine or rent him a sleazy video? He doesn't know your husband and has no grudge against him. He just wants to make money from your husband. Is he not your husband's enemy and your enemy?

What about people who want to enlist you in their causes or get your name on a petition or tell you a juicy piece of gossip or pass on a racial stereotype? If they simply want to use you for their own purposes, they are not concerned about your eternal nature or the quality of your relationship with your Heavenly Father. Without any malice toward you personally, they may be acting out of enmity.

Amulek continues: "Pour out your souls in your closets, and your secret places, and in your wilderness.

"Yea, and when you do not cry unto the Lord, let your hearts be full, drawn out in prayer unto him continually for your welfare, and also for the welfare of those who are around you" (Alma 34:20–27).

Don't we have a need to understand our world and our generations? In our sphere and in our times, our need for revelation and clear vision is just as great as Enoch's need was. And it is my testimony that the Lord is just as willing to grant us that revelation in answer to our prayers as he was to answer Enoch's prayer.

Let me tell you one story that illustrates this point. A woman named Brenda was on her way to the hospital to visit Donald, a quadriplegic who had been paralyzed by falling from a ladder. She stopped at the supermarket on her way to pick up a few things and accidentally, in her hurry, bumped into a display of shoelaces. She felt very embarrassed and hastily picked things up. As a way of making amends, she dropped one package of shoelaces into her cart and paid for them with her groceries, but put them in her purse rather than leaving them in the sack with the rest of the groceries. Then, she writes, this happened:

"That day Donald was unusually despondent. 'Brenda,' he said, 'Sometimes I feel as though God simply doesn't care anymore.'

"'You know he cares,' I began. But I had no real answer for him. We sat in silence.

"'Oh, by the way,' Donald said as I started to leave, 'the nurse broke one of my shoestrings. Could you get me a new pair?' [Can you imagine how Brenda felt when Donald made this request?] She writes:

"I opened my purse and took out the packet from the supermarket. . . . I laced them into Donald's shoes.

"Shoestrings! For a pair of shoes on feet that could not move to wear them out. For a set of hands that couldn't even tie the bow.

"'Donald, if God cares enough to supply you with shoestrings even before you ask,' I said, 'I'm certain he cares enough about you in more important ways.'

"A smile broke onto his face. 'Yes, you're right,' Donald said. 'I'm sure too.'

"Shoestrings [marvels Brenda]. Whenever I'm discouraged, I think of them. Then I know that God cares for me too. Right down to the laces in my shoes."[1]

Think about it. The God who can see that Brenda walks out of a store with a pair of shoelaces she doesn't need, to provide comfort to Donald in his discouragement, is watching over you with the same tenderness and the same love.

The Lord's Love

So that's the first great moment from Enoch's vision. The second is how much the Lord loves us, as shown by his weeping over the wickedness of his children. To me, this is one of the most moving passages of scripture. A chilling part of Enoch's vision was the revelation that "the power of Satan was upon all the face of the earth." The scripture says:

"And [Enoch] beheld Satan; and he had a great chain in his hand, and it veiled the whole face of the earth with darkness; and he looked up and laughed, and his angels rejoiced. . . .

"And . . . the God of heaven looked upon the residue of the people, and he wept; . . .

"And Enoch said unto the Lord: How is it that thou canst weep, seeing thou art holy, and from all eternity to all eternity?

"And were it possible that man could number the particles of the earth, yea, millions of earths like this, it would not be a beginning to the number of thy creations; and thy curtains are stretched out still; . . .

"And . . . from all eternity to all eternity . . . naught but peace, justice, and truth is the habitation of thy throne; and mercy shall go before thy face and have no end; how is it thou canst weep?" (Moses 7:26–31).

Sometimes we think that our happiness lies in changes in a few circumstances: a new job, a new car, a new dress. Enoch is saying to God: You are a perfect being. You are in a perfect place. All of your works are perfect. How is it possible for you to feel sorrow under these circumstances? But Enoch has not understood that God's perfection lies in the perfection of his love and the perfection of his respect for moral agency. As a result, Heavenly Father cannot see the suffering that any of his children will bring upon themselves through their willful disobedience without feeling sorrow even to the point of weeping. The sacred and mighty law of agency means that he can only invite and command and hold out a vision of possibilities to us. He can never compel or force our obedience.

The Lord explained to Enoch: "Behold, these thy brethren; they are the workmanship of mine own hands, and I gave unto them their knowledge, in the day I created them; and in the Garden of Eden, gave I unto man his agency; And unto thy brethren have I said, and also given commandment, that they should love one another, and that they should choose me, their Father; but behold [and please pay attention to this. It is a terrible, terrible accusation that the Lord brings against the disobedient], they are without affection, and they hate their own blood; . . . I can stretch forth mine hands and hold all the creations which I have made; and mine eye can pierce them also, . . . But behold, . . . Satan shall be their father, and misery shall be their doom; and the whole heavens shall weep over them, even all the workmanship of mine hands; wherefore should not the heavens weep, seeing these shall suffer?" (Moses 7:32–33; 36–37).

Think of the power of that love! Sometimes we may feel discouraged in the face of the magnitude and extent of the evil with which we must deal. But Enoch's vision reminds us that God watches over us and yearns for us and that Jesus is our advocate with the Father—not just at the Judgment Day, but every day.

I was very touched by the experience of a woman who had been recently widowed and who had spent a very restless and troubled night. I know what those nights feel like, and I'm sure that those of you who have also been bereaved, whether of a spouse or a parent or a child, know the same feeling of longing for the night to end but dreading the dawn because you have so few resources with which to meet it. This woman said that she "felt too weary to pray for [her]self" and could only sigh, "Lord, . . . I need someone to pray *for* me right now." She writes:

"Almost instantly God's Spirit comforted my distraught mind with the words of Hebrews 7:25: ['Wherefore he is able also to save them to the uttermost that come unto God by him, seeing he ever liveth to make intercession for them.'] Think of that! Jesus is always praying for us in the presence of our Heavenly Father!"

This insight brought immediate comfort to this lonely and weary widow. She writes:

"[I was reminded] that Jesus was praying for me that very moment. With a wave of relief, I acknowledged Him as my lifelong intercessor. I will never forget how that bleak morning became gold-tinged with hope. Since then, I have drawn courage and strength countless times from my faithful High Priest."[2]

But the lessons from Enoch's experience do not end there. As the Lord explained the cause of his grief to Enoch, the prophet had a comparable experience to the Lord's. "Wherefore Enoch knew, and looked upon their wickedness, and their misery, and wept and stretched forth his arms, and his heart swelled wide as eternity; and his bowels yearned; and all eternity shook" (Moses 7:41).

We are not called to bear the prophet's burden of knowledge; but we cannot avoid a similar burden for our own times and in our own circumstances. There are about us human beings who have been raised in such abysmal circumstances and under such brutal conditions that they "are without affection, and they hate their own blood" (Moses 7:33).

Where are the tears for their misery? Where are the

outstretched arms, the heart wide as eternity, the yearning? As we strive to understand things from God's point of view, we will also feel God's compassion for the suffering and desire to do all we can to alleviate it.

Mother Teresa said something very profound that I think sheds some light on this topic: "Material suffering is suffering from hunger, suffering from homelessness, from all kinds of disease, but I still think that the greatest suffering is being lonely, feeling unloved, just having no one. I have come more and more to realize that it is being unwanted that is the worst disease that any human being can ever experience."[3]

But the solution is also inherent in the experience of Enoch. When he sees the broken-heartedness of God and understands the reason, then he also cannot refrain from weeping, and his own heart stretches wide to encompass those who will bring that suffering and misery upon themselves through their wickedness. To the extent that we see and understand the plan of God, we will also feel his love for everyone and share the anguish he feels when people use their free agency to turn away from that gift.

We've discussed two points of Enoch's vision: his seeing God face to face, and his understanding the preciousness of each soul, as God understands it.

The Earth's Soul

The third important aspect of Enoch's vision is the understanding he gained that the earth has a soul that is capable of being grieved because of the pollution and wickedness of its inhabitants.

"Enoch looked upon the earth; and he heard a voice from the bowels thereof, saying: Wo, wo is me, the mother of men; I am pained, I am weary, because of the wickedness of my children. When shall I rest, and be cleansed from the filthiness which is gone forth out of me? When will my Creator sanctify me, that I may rest, and righteousness for a season abide upon my face?

"And when Enoch heard the earth mourn, he wept, and cried unto the Lord, saying: O Lord, wilt thou not have compassion upon the earth?" (Moses 7:48–49).

The context in which this scripture was given was the wickedness of the earth at the time of Noah. I've heard some people say this scripture refers to the chemical pollution that we have inflicted on the earth in the last half of the twentieth century. I don't know that the scripture lends itself exactly to that reading; but I certainly *do* think it's true that, when we know that the earth has a spirit of its own and is grieved for wickedness, it makes us think twice about acts of disrespect— about throwing trash and litter around, about the wanton killing of animals and birds, about contaminating water, poisoning plants, and destroying forests, about being wasteful and careless.

Hopefully, we've all become more aware of living more simply, of restricting our use of nonrenewable resources, and of recycling. There are probably ways we could all do better and should do better, but I think one of the most important things we can do is to realize that human beings don't own this planet. We *share* this planet with all the rest of God's creations. I was really charmed to read an account by a writer named Marilyn Meberg, who was visiting her daughter in beautiful Pacific Grove, California. As they were driving down the street, she was startled to see a sign reading: "CAUTION, BUTTERFLY ZONE." She was intrigued and puzzled.

"Beth, did you see that butterfly sign? What on earth does

it mean? Is it for real? Why does one need to be cautious about butterflies? Are they hostile?"

Beth explained to her mother that Pacific Grove is one of the few migratory destinations in the world for the monarch butterfly and that during October and November each year thousands of them make an 1800-mile trek to various groves of trees in the area where Beth and her mother were driving. The signs were intended to prevent the butterflies from being needlessly injured or killed.

Marilyn later learned that there was even a city ordinance that mandates punishment by a heavy fine for anyone caught hurting or interfering in any way with the safety of the butterflies.

Reflecting on the community's tender commitment to preserve the delicate and gorgeous creatures, Marilyn Meberg wrote: "[It] made my insides smile and go soft."[4]

I think such concerns for one of God's creations must bring a moment of rest and peace to Mother Earth.

The City of Enoch

We've considered three aspects of the vision of Enoch: the literal appearance of God in answer to prayer; the love the Lord has for his children, which is so immense that he weeps as he sees our wickedness; and the fact that the earth has a soul that is grieved by human wickedness. You remember that I began by indicating that I liked the story of Enoch because it was a story with a happy ending, and you're probably thinking, *Well, this doesn't sound all that happy to me!* But now we're coming to the happy part. Despite all the wickedness, despite the great misery, despite the enmity and the violence, it was in the midst of such corruption that the righteous city of Enoch was established.

The scriptures describe the amazing event this way: "The Lord came and dwelt with his people, and they dwelt in righteousness.

" . . . And the Lord blessed the land, and they were blessed upon the mountains, and upon the high places, and did flourish.

"And the Lord called his people Zion, because they were of one heart and one mind, and dwelt in righteousness; and there was no poor among them.

"And . . . [the city] was called the City of Holiness, even Zion.

"And after that Zion was taken up into heaven" (Moses 7:16–19, 23).

You might ask, how is such a thing possible? How can human beings create a situation where they are of one heart and of one mind? Given all of the diversity in our thoughts, feelings, opinions, and circumstances, isn't such a thing impossible? And even if it could happen, wouldn't it be undesirable? Who would want to live in a place where everybody thought alike and felt the same way? Wouldn't that be even more regimented than being in a very strict army?

Ah, but that's not what the scripture says. It doesn't say that everybody was the same or even that they behaved the same. It says "they were of one heart and one mind" because of "the glory of the Lord which was upon his people" and his dwelling in their midst. Since he was there, it seems obvious that the people of Enoch were following the counsel that the Lord also gave to the Saints in Joseph Smith's day. He said: "Behold, the Lord requireth the heart and a willing mind; and the willing and obedient shall eat the good of the land of Zion in these last days" (D&C 64:34). It seems significant that these instructions were given in the same context, in both Joseph Smith's day and in the time of Enoch—the process of establishing Zion.

And that's the explanation of how we can be of one heart and one mind. We don't have to be glancing sideways to see how our neighbors are doing and whether we're in step with them or they're in step with us. When we have our hearts fixed on the Savior—when we have given our hearts to the Savior—and when our minds are willing to receive his instructions, then we can truly be one, no matter how different we are as individuals and no matter how many different things the Savior is instructing us to do in our individual stewardships. We will all be part of the same whole.

This is the point the Apostle Paul makes. Comparing the Church to the human body, he reminds us that each individual part has its unique function and is needed: The body of Christ needs heads and hearts and hands. It needs noses and toes and eyes and ears (see 1 Corinthians 12:12–21). No one needs to be offended or upset or worried because someone has a different assignment. If we each do the tasks that lie before us with our might, we will be helping everybody.

Elder Robert E. Sackley, one of the few General Authorities to literally die on the job (during the time he was serving as a member of the Australian Area presidency) took very seriously the Lord's assignment to feed the hungry and minister to the ill. He says: "We can't all go to Africa to help dig wells or nurse dying children, nor can we all go on welfare missions. But each of us can be more loving and tolerant. We can eliminate the prejudice and bigotry from our own souls, realizing that we truly are a global family."[5]

Let me conclude with one more beautiful thought that has

come to us from Enoch. I like to think of this as a one-verse description of the plan of salvation. The Lord explains to Enoch: "By reason of transgression cometh the fall, which fall bringeth death, and inasmuch as ye were born into the world by water, and blood, and the spirit, which I have made, and so became of dust a living soul, even so ye must be born again into the kingdom of heaven, of water, and of the Spirit, and be cleansed by blood, even the blood of mine Only Begotten; that ye might be sanctified from all sin, and enjoy the words of eternal life in this world, and eternal life in the world to come, even immortal glory" (Moses 6:59).

That is the vision that Enoch holds out to us: that we might partake of "the words of eternal life in this world, and eternal life in the world to come, even immortal glory." It is my sincere prayer that we will cherish that vision and work with all our strength to bring about Zion.

NOTES

1. Brenda Minner, "His Mysterious Ways," *Guideposts*, March 1995, 15.

2. Joanie E. Yoder, "Our Fulltime Intercessor," *Our Daily Bread*, March, April, May 1995.

3. Mother Teresa, *In the Heart of the World*, edited by Becky Benenate (Novato, California: New World Library, 1997), 14.

4. Marilyn Meberg, "Ten Thousand Butterflies—Maybe More," in *Joy Breaks* (Grand Rapids, Michigan: Zondervan Publishing House, 1997), 27–28.

5. Derin Head Rodriguez, *From Every Nation* (Salt Lake City: Deseret Book Co., 1990), 173.

BIBLIOGRAPHY

Bachelder, Louise, ed. *Golden Words of Faith, Hope, and Love*. Mount Vernon, Virginia: Peter Pauper Press, 1969.

Baumann, Ellyn. *Daily Guideposts, 1994*. Carmel, New York: Guideposts, 1993.

Bellarmine, St. Robert, and Jean Pierre Camus. *The New Book of Christian Quotations*. Compiled by Tony Castle. New York: Crossroads, 1983.

Bender, Sue. *Everyday Sacred: A Woman's Journey Home*. New York: HarperCollins Publishers, 1995.

Brown, H. Jackson, Jr., comp. *Live and Learn and Pass It On*, vol. 2. Nashville: Rutledge Hill Press, 1955.

Brussat, Frederic, and Mary Ann Brussat, eds. *Spiritual Literacy: Reading the Sacred in Everyday Life*. New York: Simon and Schuster, 1996.

Cameron, Julia. *Heart Steps*. New York: Jeremy P. Tarcher/Putnam, 1997.

Castle, Tony, comp. *The New Book of Christian Quotations*. New York: Crossroads, 1983.

Chicken Soup for the Christian Soul: 101 Stories to Open the Heart and Rekindle the Spirit. Compiled by Jack Canfield, Mark Victor Hansen, Patty Aubery, and Nancy Mitchell. Deerfield Beach, Florida: Health Communications, Inc., 1997.

Condie, Spencer J. *Your Agency: Handle with Care*. Salt Lake City: Bookcraft, 1996.

Edelman, Marian Wright. *Guide My Feet: Prayers and Meditations* on *Loving and Working for Children*. Boston: Beacon Press, 1995.

Encyclopedia of Mormonism. 4 vols. New York: Macmillan Publishing Company, 1992.

Evely, Louis. *Listen to Love: Reflections on the Seasons of the Year; Photographs, Poems and Readings*. Compiled by Louis M. Savary with Thomas J. O'Connor, Ruth M. Cullen, and Diane M. Plummer. New York: Regina Press, 1971.

Fulghum, Robert. *All I Really Need to Know I Learned in Kindergarten*. New York: Ivy Books, 1986.

Griessman, Gene. *The Words Lincoln Lived By*. New York: Fireside, 1997.

Halberstam, Yitta, and Judith Leventhal. *Small Miracles*. Holbrook, Massachussetts: Adams Media Corporation, 1997.

Heller, David. *Dear God*. New York: Berkeley Publishing Group, 1987.

A Heritage of Faith: Talks Selected from the BYU Women's Conferences. Edited by Mary E. Stovall and Carol Cornwall Madsen. Salt Lake City: Deseret Book, 1988.

Holy Humor. Edited by Cal Samara and Rose Samara. Carmel, California: Guideposts, 1996.

Holzapfel, Jeni Broberg, and Richard Nietzel Holzapfel. *Sisters at the Well: Women and the Life and Teachings of Jesus*. Salt Lake City: Bookcraft, 1993.

Joy Breaks. Grand Rapids, Michigan: Zondervan Publishing House, 1997.

Kimball, Spencer W. *Faith Precedes the Miracle*. Salt Lake City: Deseret Book, 1977.

Kushner, Harold S. *How Good Do We Have to Be?* Boston: Little, Brown and Company, 1996.

Liddle, Theron C., ed. *A Thought for Today*. Salt Lake City: Deseret News Press, 1961.

Lindbergh, Anne Morrow. *Gift from the Sea*. New York: Vintage
    Books, 1977.

Millet, Robert L. *When a Child Wanders*. Salt Lake City: Deseret
    Book, 1996.

Morrison, Alexander B. *The Dawning of a Brighter Day: The Church
    in Black Africa*. Salt Lake City: Deseret Book, 1990.

Mother Teresa. *In the Heart of the World*. Edited by Becky
    Benenate. Novato, California: New World Library, 1997.

Our Daily Bread. Grand Rapids, Michigan: RBC Ministries, 1996.

Peterson, Wilferd A. *More about the Art of Living*. New York:
    Fireside, 1997.

Random Acts of Kindness. Berkeley, California: Conari Press, 1993.

Rodriguez, Derin Head. *From Every Nation*. Salt Lake City: Deseret
    Book, 1990.

Smith, Joseph. *History of the Church of Jesus Christ of Latter-day
    Saints, Period I*. Salt Lake City: Deseret Book, 1974.

Sunset with God. Tulsa, Oklahoma: Honor Books, 1996.

Thayne, Emma Lou. *As For Me and My House*. Salt Lake City:
    Bookcraft, 1989.

*To Your Success: Thoughts to Give Wings to Your Work and Your
    Dreams*. Compiled by Dan Zadra. Woodinville, Washington:
    Compendium, Incorporated, 1994.

Walk the World Proudly. New York: Doubleday & Company, 1969.

Walsh, Len. *Read Japanese Today*. Rutland, Vermont, and Tokyo:
    Charles E. Tuttle Co., 1969.

INDEX